Crewel
creatures

Fresh ideas
for Jacobean
embroidery

Crewel

Fresh ideas
for Jacobean
embroidery

creatures

HAZEL Blomkamp

SEARCH PRESS

ACKNOWLEDGEMENTS & THANKS

Louise Grimbeek, Sandra Kloppers, Margie Breetzke and Alexandra Cullen for proof stitching the designs in this book;

Pat van Wyk and Melanie Shrives for keeping the studio running while I took the time to write this book;

Di van Niekerk for the use of her beautiful studio during the photoshoot and, along with Wilsia Metz, for friendship and support.

This book is dedicated to
the memory of Ivan Naudé,
a gentleman and a genius.

First published in Great Britain 2018
Search Press Limited
Wellwood, North Farm Road,
Tunbridge Wells, Kent, TN2 3DR

Originally published in South Africa in 2018 by
Metz Press, 1 Cameronians Ave, Welgemoed
7530, South Africa

ISBN 978 178221 5257

Publisher   Wilsia Metz
Design and layout   Liezl Maree
Proofreader   Glynne Newlands
Illustrations   Hazel Blomkamp
Photographer   Kenny Irvine,
                     Di van Niekerk
Printed and bound by WKT Company, China

Contents

Introduction

Some years ago, walking through a quaint and arty area in Montreal, I spotted a painting of an owl in the window of an art gallery. He was largely made up of metal parts but what really stopped me in my tracks was the clock face that was his pot belly.

It inspired me. It just did and for hours I found myself thinking about how I could translate that idea into embroidery. By the time I got home from Canada I knew exactly what I wanted to do and the moment I was over my jet lag, I sat down and drew an owl with Jacobean flowers in his belly.

It started me on a most enjoyable journey and inevitably, whilst stitching Owlfred (as he later became known) it dawned on me that the journey doesn't have to end with him. Why stop at an owl? What about other animals?

This book is the result.

There are so many animals that could be given a crewel or Jacobean treatment but, living in Africa, I decided that I would like to concentrate on animals that live on my own continent and, moreover, that I would like to do them in the colours of Africa.

These colours are usually represented as the bright orange of the sunsets, or the primary colours of Ndebele art. They are so much more than that. The khaki of some of the grasses, or the gold of those same grasses in winter, the purple of distant mountains, the grey of the sky when there is a storm brewing, desert shades, blue skies and the many shades to be found in the wild flowers, particularly in the spring. I could wax lyrical for pages about the colours in an African

landscape. Suffice to say, that it is colourful and it is probably safe to state that not a single shade goes unrepresented. Even white because sometimes, very rarely, it snows.

In this book you will find:

- **Norman the tortoise**. Normally a rather dull creature, the shell of a tortoise provides a canvas for Jacobean embellishment which, in turn, makes this tortoise colourful and fanciful.
- **Audrey the ostrich**. Also a reasonably colourless creature, I chose to work Audrey in the colours of the Klein Karoo, a semi-desert region of Southern Africa and home to many ostrich farms.
- **Maureen the owl**. This project is big. I wanted to do an owl in full flight, about to pounce on the rat that ate my Internet cables at about the time I was considering the design. If the Jacobean elements in the bird were going to show up at all, then they could not be too small. The result is that overall, the bird is big. Satisfying though.
- **Janet the snake**. Although snakes feature in many old Jacobean Tree of Life pieces, is not usually a subject that would be embroidered nowadays, mostly because people have a primal fear of snakes. Including me. They are, however, rather beautiful creatures with the hood of the cobra being the perfect place to play with Jacobean embellishment. Despite being a person who lifts her feet off the floor when snakes are discussed – in case one chooses to slither past – I enjoyed the stitching of this project possibly more than the others. She has a smiling face, the pearls make her pretty and there is a wide and interesting combination of stitches in the lower coil.

- **Shirley the elephant**. The population of these giants of the jungle decreases every year, partly because they are hunted for their ivory and partly because as human populations increase in Africa and Asia, there is less territory left for elephants. I am privileged to have come across many elephants in my life and it saddens me to think that in years to come they may no longer exist. Shirley is a fanciful depiction of an African elephant – because she has big ears. Asian elephants have smaller ears.
- **Roger the rhino**. Owing to the myth of aphrodisiacal properties in the horn of the rhinoceros, this species is on the critically endangered list. On an almost daily basis there will be mention on our local television news of rhinos slaughtered. Despite the energy and funds that go into stopping the poaching of these magnificent animals, the numbers decrease steadily.

Animals have personalities, feelings and emotions. I have tried to convey some of that in these projects. They are as deserving of a given name as a human being and, because I am really just a sentimental old thing, I named them after the Boxer puppies in a litter born to my precious dogs last year – each one with its own distinct personality. Whilst one is not able to get to know a wild animal in the same way that one would a precious family pet, I have a sneaking suspicion that these animals have similar quirks and characters.

I hope you enjoy working on these projects. I have certainly had fun.

HAZEL *Blomkamp*

General tips before starting

YOU MUST BE ABLE TO SEE PROPERLY

One of the most common inhibiting factors for embroiderers, especially those of a certain age and older, is being able to see properly. This is of importance when one is doing fine work and there is a lot of that in this book.

Optometrists' machines are set to magnify at about waist level. This does not work for embroidery because you will generally hold your work at chest level. When you visit your optometrist, take a piece of your work with you so that your spectacles can be made to suit your working style.

The best spectacles are bi- or multi-focals with a small spot in the bottom part of the lenses made to magnify, by two or three times, at chest level. Alternatively, you can have your optometrist make you a dedicated pair of spectacles for needlework. I have a pair of those and they're not pretty. The lenses are so thick that they look like the bottom of whisky glasses. So what. They work and that's the main thing.

There are times, though, when even those are not enough and that is when I put on a second pair. That is, a pair of plus 1.5 readers in front of the whisky glasses. This creates a telescope and is more comfortable than grappling with one of those magnifying glasses that hang around your neck, or craning your neck to look through a beauticians' magnifying light. If you are travelling, this system works very well. So little to take with you.

GOOD LIGHT

You don't want to have to restrict yourself to only being able to work during daylight hours, so you will need a good light or lights.

Over the years I've tried just about every single lighting system out there and have now gone back to basics. Two inexpensive metal angle-poise lamps fitted with 15-watt energy saver bulbs. They are set up on either side of me as I stitch. Because they are angle-poise, I pull them closer or push them away, depending on what I am stitching. This really is the best lighting system for me.

And here's the thing. My life is filled with mad and crazy big dogs who knock things over. If they destroy either of these very affordable lights, it doesn't hurt quite so much when I have to buy a replacement.

TRANSFERRING YOUR DESIGN

The line drawings for all the designs in this book are at the back. The easiest way to transfer them onto your fabric is with dressmaker's carbon. Like most things in life, I do what works best for me. And dressmaker's carbon, or chalk paper, is my choice.

1. Make a photocopy of the drawing, adjusting the size where recommended;
2. Pin the photocopy to the fabric, taking care to place it in the centre. Don't get too fussy about the grain, just get it as straight as you can;
3. Place a sheet of dressmaker's carbon, ink side down, between the photocopy and the fabric;
4. Using the hard tip of a ballpoint pen – preferably one that has no ink in it (I have a dry pen in my toolbox for this task) – go over each and every line, pressing hard. And I do mean pressing hard. You should end up with a sore finger. If you don't press hard enough, the lines won't transfer.

Another alternative is to pin the photocopy to the underside of the fabric. Place it on a light box and trace the lines on with a pencil, a blue washout pen, or a Pilot Frixion pen.

And if the above is all too much for you, order a print pack from our website (hazelblomkamp.com)!

PENS

If you have transferred your design with chalk paper, you may find that the lines fade. This is because as you stitch, your hand rubs over those lines taking some of the chalk off every time. It is advisable to draw over those lines with either a blue washout pen or a Pilot Frixion pen.

The blue washout pen is controversial because it has been known to cause brown lines that won't wash out. Brown lines and stains can be avoided if you follow two simple guidelines:

- Always rinse your embroidery in cold water before putting it into any detergent;
- Do not allow the lines to fade. If you draw something onto fabric with a washout pen, grow bored with it and put it away in a cupboard for a while, when you come back to it those lines will have faded to brown and you won't get rid of them.

Provided you avoid the above, you can use a washout pen with impunity.

The Frixion pen is fairly new on the market and I have to say that, until recently, I had resisted using it. I was taken in by the idea that the chemicals in the ink may cause damage to the fabric a hundred years down the line. Well, who cares. I'm long gone by then and what is more important is that I need to use something that works well today. And this pen works very nicely thank you.

The lines come out when you apply heat and pressing the fabric with an iron is generally advised. I find, however, that a hair dryer works better.

It has become my favourite pen.

HOOPS AND FRAMES

I reject so-called rules when it comes to any kind of creativity. I do think, though, that if there has to be any single rule for embroidery, it is that you must work in a hoop or frame. It improves the tension of your work and for many of the techniques it prevents the fabric from puckering. You cannot produce good work without them.

The projects in this book use:
• The Morgan no-slip hoop 12" and 14" lap stand;
• A 30" heavy duty scroll frame;
• Edmunds stretcher bars of varying lengths.

The type of hoop or frame used is mentioned in the general notes at the beginning of the instructions for each project.

GRIME GUARDS

No matter how often you wash your hands, or how clean you keep your working environment, a grubby ring is likely to form at the place where the fabric meets the outer ring of the hoop. To avoid this problem, make a fabric guard.

Measure the circumference of your hoop. Add 50 mm (2") for a small hoop and 100 mm (4") for a large hoop. Using that measurement, cut a strip of fabric that is 250 mm (10") wide.

Fold the strip in half, with right sides together, and sew a seam to join the ends of the strip, making it into a tube.

Stitch a 15 mm (⅔") casing by turning in a hem at the top and bottom.

Calculate how much narrow elastic you will need by tightly stretching a piece around the circumference of the hoop and adding 25 mm (1"). Cut two pieces and thread them into the top and bottom casings, stitch them together and close the gaps of the casings.

Once you have stretched the working fabric into the hoop, stretch the grime guard around the perimeter of the hoop, protecting the edge of the embroidery, and tucking the excess working fabric on the outside of the hoop into the part of that grime guard the lies below the hoop.

USE A THREAD CONDITIONER

It strengthens your thread, makes silk and rayon threads less lively and delays the stripping of metallic thread. It certainly prevents tangles and knotting when you are working with long pieces of beading thread.

Beeswax is good, but the best is a silicone thread conditioner. This leaves no residue.

THE WONDERS OF SUPER GLUE

I don't like using a thimble but find that a hole develops in the tip of the finger that I use to push the needle through the fabric. It is very sore if I happen to push the needle on that spot which, inevitably I always do. I place a blob of super glue on the pad of my middle finger and hold it in the air for a few minutes. Once that blob is dry it will be rock hard and a needle will not penetrate it. It peels off after a few hours. Ignore the neurotics who predict dire health problems. They're wrong. I've used it for years and I've never had to go to the emergency room.

START AND END YOUR THREADS WITH A KNOT

We do needlework for our pleasure, not to be judged. Whilst the back of your work should not look like a bird's nest, it does not have to look the same as the front. It really doesn't. This is the 21st century.

THE STITCHES IN THIS BOOK

Like all girls of my generation, I learnt embroidery at school and from older members of my family. Since then I have developed in my own way, working stitches and techniques to achieve the look I want as opposed to conforming to what somebody else tells me I should be doing. The way that I have worked the stitches and techniques in this book are illustrated and described in the techniques' galleries. If you have been taught or have learnt differently, then you should use the way that works best for you. This applies, in particular, to long and short stitch shading. Do each stitch in a way that works best for you.

SLOW AND METHODICAL IS THE BEST WAY

It is important to remember that, as mentioned above, we do needlework for pleasure. I enjoy the journey that is each design I stitch and when I reach my destination, I am often bereft.

Focus on the pleasure of working each square inch, aiming for it to be as perfect as you can possibly make it. If a stitch is not sitting at the right angle, take it out before you move on. The same with beads. If you don't do that, others may not notice but you will. Every time you look at it.

Enjoy watching each part come alive before your eyes.

WASHING YOUR EMBROIDERY

We are living in the 21st century with good dyes and non-shrinking fabrics. You can wash your needlework. Provided you have checked that all the dyes are colour-fast – which they should be if you have used good quality thread – you MUST wash it. It brings the colours to life and the sheen of the thread reappears.

- Rinse it well in cold water to get rid of any lines that you may have drawn with a washout pen.
- Soak it for a few hours in tepid water mixed with a tablespoon or two of good detergent.
- Swish it around a bit before rinsing it in cold water.
- If you find there are marks – perhaps chalk paper lines – that haven't washed out, scrub them gently with pure soap on a toothbrush.
- Rinse again to make sure that no soap or detergent remains.
- Squeeze out the excess water, place it flat on a towel and roll up the towel.
- Squeeze the towel with the embroidery inside it to get rid of any remaining excess water.
- Stretch the damp embroidery in a hoop or frame that is larger than the embroidered area and place it in front of an open window, out of direct sunlight, to dry in the breeze.
- If you have stretched it well you will probably not need to iron it when it is dry. If you do need to iron it, turn it wrong side up on a folded towel and press the back with an iron set on medium heat.

Materials

FABRICS

200 gsm 45/55 Linen Cotton blend

All of the projects in this book have been worked on a 200 gsm 45/55 linen cotton blend. The subject matter of this book told me that I needed to use a natural coloured fabric and because I intend to frame them, I required a medium weight fabric that could be stretched for framing without creating too much bulk.

You may choose to work on a different colour or a different fabric. My preference is for fabric that comprises natural fibres but, having said that, I can picture Janet the Snake on the back of a jacket. That jacket could be made of any of a wide range of fabrics. The rule of thumb is only that the fabric should be stable, washable and strong enough to accommodate the stitches and beadwork.

Cotton voile

Each project lists cotton voile backing fabric. By backing your base fabric with voile, you provide stability and give yourself a place to end off the thread. Lightweight and smooth cotton voile in either white, off-white or ecru is the perfect fabric to use. It is unlikely to shrink but you should take the precaution of rinsing it in cold water before you use it. Once it is dry and pressed, cut a piece to the same size as the embroidery fabric, tack (baste) the two pieces together with horizontal and vertical lines through the middle and machine stitch around the edges to prevent fraying.

THREADS AND THEIR NEEDLES

When embroidering, you should endeavour to use quality threads. Their dyes should be colour-fast, they should not break easily and should not develop fluff-balls while you are working with them. The threads used in this book are available worldwide and largely fulfil the criteria mentioned above.

Any country that signed up to the 1997 Kyoto Protocol undertook to, amongst other things, ban certain toxic chemicals in the dyes that are used in textiles. This means that it has become impossible to guarantee colour-fastness in any fabric or thread. Whilst many thread manufacturers still claim that their threads are colour-fast, this is not strictly correct, particularly with regard to the darker reds, greens and purples.

It is advisable to check all threads before use by dipping a small length into hot water, then dabbing it dry on a white towel. If no colour comes out it is good to use. If colours do run then dunk the whole skein into the hot water, dabbing it dry and repeating this process until the white towel stays white.

Stranded cotton

Usually six stranded, this thread comes in skeins of 8 m (8¾ yd). It has a lustrous sheen and you can embroider with as many strands as you wish, depending on the texture you wish to achieve. It is ideal for fine work. This book uses stranded cotton from the DMC and Chameleon ranges. For the projects in this book, use a size 7 or 10 embroidery needle when stitching with stranded cotton.

Perle thread

This twisted thread is available in a variety of sizes and colours, with a sheen that is remarkably effective. It is easy to work with and provides alternative texture to your work. It is ideal for many of the weaving and needle-lace stitches featured and this book uses thread from the DMC, Lizbeth and Presencia ranges of Perle threads. Because of the twist it is inclined to tangle. To guard against this, run it through a thread conditioner. Use a size 7 embroidery needle, a size 26 chenille or a size 26 tapestry needle when stitching with Perle thread.

Fine cordonette thread

This book uses DMC Special Dentelles 80 for the finer needle lace and weaving stitches. Similar to Perle, it is a twisted thread with a light sheen. As with perle thread, because of the twist it is inclined to tangle. To guard against this, run it through a thread conditioner. Use a size 7 embroidery needle or a size 26 tapestry needle when stitching with special dentelles.

Metallic thread

Although manufactured from polyester yarn, metallic threads have the appearance of metal and are guaranteed to add an exciting dimension to your work, particularly when used in conjunction with beads. These threads shred easily so you should work with short pieces and re-thread often. Thread conditioner provides lubrication and protection, so should be used. This book uses metallic thread from the Madeira Metallic and DMC Diamant ranges. You should use a size 7 embroidery needle or a size 22 chenille when stitching with metallic threads.

Silk ribbon

Soft and sublime, these ribbons are made from pure silk and are available in a variety of widths. This book uses 2 mm and 4 mm Di van Niekerk hand-painted ribbons to weave an extra dimension into some of the needle-lace fillings. Because silk ribbon is reasonably fragile and damages easily, you should work with short pieces on a size 24 or 26 tapestry needle.

Beading thread

Made from nylon, these threads are all but unbreakable, perfect for working with beads that need to be worked with a tight tension. This book uses size AA C-Lon beading thread in a variety of colours to work the three-dimensional flowers and leaves that feature in most of the projects. Use either a size 10 or 12 long beading needle or a shorter size 11 sharps needle. You can also use a size 10 or 12 bead embroidery needle when working with beads. It is vitally important to check for colour-fastness.

BEADS AND CRYSTALS

Seed beads

When adding beads to your embroidery, endeavour to seek out the best beads that you can find. Using inferior quality beads ruins the effect of your work. Seed beads come from many countries and many different factories. Many of them are badly shaped, of uneven sizing and with holes that are off-centre. The best beads come from Japan and this book uses beads from the Miyuki range of Japanese seed beads.

Bead sizing is determined by the number of beads that fit into an inch which means that, like counted thread linen, the higher the number, the smaller the bead. In this book, the projects use size 15° and size 11° Delica beads, size 15°, size 11° and size 8° round rocailles, drop beads and #1 (3 mm) bugle beads.

When incorporating beads into your embroidery stitches, attach them to fabric using stranded cotton, the colour of which should be similar to the shade of the bead. It is sometimes better, though, when attaching single beads to use a thread colour that is identical to the background fabric. It can be useful, when working with transparent beads, to attach them with a completely different coloured thread. In this way, you can alter the colour of the bead to create additional shading.

Because the holes in the beads are small and you will need to pass the needle through, sometimes more than once, you have the choice of using a bead embroidery needle or a size 11 sharps needle. My preference is for the quilting needles. They are short and bend less. All these needles have an extremely small eye so you should use only one strand of thread which you then double over for extra strength.

When working the three-dimensional flowers and leaves, use beading thread as recommended for each project, working with either a size 10 or 12 long bead-ing needle. Some people find the long needle difficult to work with so, if you prefer, use a bead embroidery or size 11 sharps needle.

Fire polished beads

Made in the Czech Republic, often metal lined or with exquisite AB finishes, these beads are good for stamens or the ends of twigs when embellishing your embroidery with three-dimensional beaded elements. This book uses 3 mm round faceted fire polished beads. You should use the beading thread as recommended for the project and choose one of the various beading needles, using whatever you find most comfortable to work with.

Glass pearls

This book uses 2 mm glass pearls from the Preciosa range, also made in the Czech Republic. They are perfectly round. When stitched into the embroidery, use a doubled-over single strand of embroidery thread and when working them into beaded elements, use beading thread, both as recommended in the project instructions. Use one of any of the beading needles.

Crystals

To be called crystal, glass must use a minimum of 24% lead or metal oxide in its manufacture. The sizing of crystal rhinestones and beads is metric and indicates either the diameter or the length of the glass object. This book uses Preciosa flat-back crystals for the eyes of five of the six creatures in this book. They are perfect for creating glinting eyes that seem to look at you, even follow you. Attaching these crystals is described in the instructions for each of the projects that uses them.

Tools

The tools required to complete the projects in this book are listed below.

CUTTING

- Large dressmaking scissors for cutting fabric;
- A rotary cutter (optional);
- Small, sharp scissors for cutting threads.

THREADS AND THEIR NEEDLES

- Embroidery/Crewel needles: Sizes 7 and 10;
- Chenille needles: Size 18 or 20
- Tapestry needles: Sizes 24 and 26;
- Quilting needles: Size 11 Sharps;
- Long beading needles: Sizes 10 and 12.

TRACING

- Dressmaker's carbon.
- Alternatively: A light box for transferring designs onto fabric used in conjunction with either a blue tailor's pen, a Pilot Frixion pen or a soft pencil.

GENERAL TOOLS

- A sewing machine and good quality thread;
- Embroidery hoops – 14";
- Scroll frames – 36";
- Stretcher bars – 12", 14", 15", 16", 18", 22";
- Thread conditioner;
- A beading mat or beading tray
- A seam ripper or stitch cutter for unpicking;
- A pair of tweezers to get rid of fluff when you are unpicking.
- A Spinster twisting tool for cord making.

Stitches & techniques

Embroidery stitches

Backstitch

Working from right to left, bring the needle up a stitch length before the end of the line you wish to stitch. Go in at the end of the line, coming up again a stitch length away from the beginning of the stitch you are working. Repeat as necessary, keeping your stitch length as even as possible.

Battlement couching

Work a layer of long, straight stitches across the area using thread shade 1. These can be vertical or diagonal. Work another layer of long, straight stitches that are placed at right angles to the first layer using the same shade. Work up to three more layers using shades 2, 3 and 4 of thread. Work small, straight couching stitches over the intersection of the last layer of trellis stitches.

Blanket stitch – double

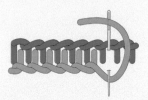

Work a line of blanket stitch (*see* page 19) leaving a small space between the stitches. When you have completed the row, turn the work around and work a line of blanket stitch that starts a fraction away from the base of the first line. Take the needle into the fabric slightly under the ridge of the first line, coming up to catch the loop a little way along from where you started, creating a blanket stitch that lies between those of the first line and allowing the ridge to form on the opposite side.

Blanket stitch – striped

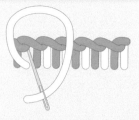

Work a line of blanket stitch (*see* page 19) leaving a small space between the stitches. When you have completed the row, work straight stitches between the blanket stitches. Start at the base and bury the needle under the ridge of the blanket stitch so that the end of each straight stitch is hidden.

Bullion knot

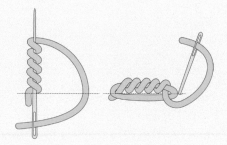

Come out of the fabric at the start of the space you wish to fill and go in again at the end of that space. Come out again at the start of the space. Leave a loop of thread on the top and don't pull the needle all the way through the fabric. Twist the thread around the needle as many times as you require. Holding the twists with the thumb and forefinger of your left hand, pull the needle through. Pull the working thread until the knot lies flat and take the needle back into the fabric at the start of the space. To make a looped bullion knot, wrap the thread more times than you need to fill the space available, so that the bullion knot will not lie completely flat but will loop up slightly.

Bullion detached chain stitch

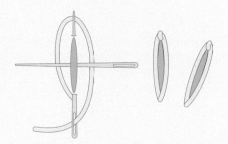

Following the guidelines for bullion knots above, work a knot of the required length. Insert a spare needle under the bullion knot as indicated in the diagram above. Bring the working needle up through the fabric just below the base of the bullion knot. Go back into the same hole coming up just above the tip of the bullion knot. Guiding the thread under both sides of the spare needle and under the tip of the working needle,

pull through. When you tighten the detached chain stitch, try to ensure that it lies slightly underneath the bullion knot. This will cause the knot to pop out a bit, making it more pronounced. Finish the detached chain stitch with a small couching stitch that catches the loop, holding it in place.

Buttonhole and blanket stitch

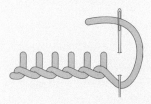

These two stitches are formed in the same way. The difference between the two is that buttonhole stitches are placed close together whilst blanket stitches have gaps between them. Working from left to right, bring the needle up on the bottom edge where you require the ridge. Take the needle in at the top edge and out again at the bottom edge, with the thread looped under the needle. Pull through and repeat as required. Secure at the end with a small couching stitch over the last one at the ridge edge.

Buttonhole circle

Come up on the outside circle. Take the needle down on the inside circle and out again on the outside circle with the loop of thread under the needle. Pull through and repeat, keeping the stitches close on the inner circle and further apart on the outside. When you meet up with where you started, complete the circle by catching the last buttonhole stitch with a couching stitch and going down where the first buttonhole stitch started.

Buttonhole flower

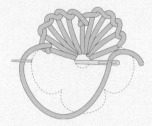

Come up on the outside in one of the valleys of the line of the flower. Take the needle down on the inside circle, and out again on the outside line, coming out of the same hole as the straight stitch you have just made. Take the needle down on the inside circle and out again on the outside line, with the loop of thread under the needle. Pull through and repeat, keeping the stitches close on the inner circle and further apart on the outside line. When you reach the bottom point of the next valley, do a small couching stitch over the buttonhole stitch you have just done. Come up again inside the buttonhole stitch in the same hole as the beginning of the couching stitch and continue working the buttonhole stitches that form the next petal. Work the small couching stitch at the bottom of each valley as this helps to define each petal. When you meet up with where you started, complete the circle by catching the last buttonhole stitch with a couching stitch and going down where the first straight stitch started.

Buttonhole stitch (layered)

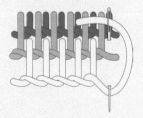

Referring to the diagram above, work your first line of buttonhole stitch as normal (dark purple). Start the next row, depicted as medium purple, slightly above the ridge of the first row. Go into the fabric at the same level that you went into the fabric when stitching the first row, coming up the bottom of the new row with the thread looped under the needle and pulling through. For the third and subsequent rows (light purple), start the row slightly above the ridge of the previous row. Go into the fabric immediately above the ridge of the first row with the thread looped under the needle and pulling through. Repeat as required.

Chain stitch

Bring the needle up on the line and pull through. Take the needle back into the same hole and come up again where you want the chain stitch to end, loop the thread under the needle and pull through. Staying inside the loop, go back into the same hole, loop the thread under the needle and pull through. Repeat as required and catch the last loop with a small couching stitch.

Chain stitch/backstitch combination

Work a row of chain stitch using shade 1. Thereafter, using shade 2, work backstitches from the middle of the first chain stitch to the space just before the start of the chain stitch. Follow that with backstitches that start in the middle of the next chain stitch and go into the start of the backstitch in the previous chain stitch. Continue doing backstitch in this way, finishing up on the outside of the last chain stitch. When you do multiple rows of this stitch combination, it is sensible

to complete the backstitch in the row before moving onto the next row of chain stitch, otherwise it is difficult to see where you should stitch if you have done all of the chain stitch before you start on the backstitch.

Couching

Use two threaded needles. Bring the first one up at the beginning of the line and lay it down. Catch it down with small stitches placed at intervals along the line. These stitches should not have a tight tension.

Cretan stitch (leaf)

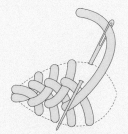

To do a cretan stitch leaf, you should work from the middle to the edge on each side, using the outline of the leaf as your guide. Starting slightly to the left of centre at the tip of the leaf, work a stitch to the right, coming up slightly to the right of centre before tightening the stitch. Work a stitch to the left, coming up slightly to the left of centre before tightening the stitch.

Detached buttonhole stitch

Surround the area that you intend to fill with small backstitches, which will be what you use to anchor the detached buttonhole stitch. Bring your needle up on the side, as indicated in the diagram, go over and under the first horizontal backstitch and, making sure that the working thread is under the needle, pull through to form a buttonhole stitch. Snake through the vertical backstitches at the end of the row. The second and subsequent rows are anchored in the loops between the stitches.

Detached chain (Lazy daisy)

Bring the needle up on the line and pull through. Take the needle back into the same hole and come up again where you want the stitch to end, loop the thread under the needle and pull through. Catch the loop with a small couching stitch.

Double detached chain

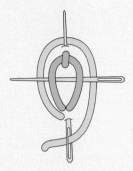

Work the smaller detached chain using the darker thread. Place a tapestry needle under the two sides of the main part of the stitch as indicated in the diagram. Using the lighter thread, come up below the first detached chain. Take the needle back into the same hole and manipulate it so that it comes out where you will want to catch the loop with the small couching stitch. Make the threads of the loop lie under both sides of the horizontal needle and, also, the needle that will catch it. Tighten the stitch, work the small couching stitch to catch the loop and remove the horizontal needle, making sure that the inner detached chain remains slightly raised in the middle.

Feather stitch (basic)

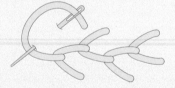

Come up on the left of the line and go in on the line, coming up immediately below that on the line and catching the loop before you tighten the stitch. Go in on the right of the line and come up on the line, catching the loop before you tighten the stitch. Go in to the left of the line and come up below the on the line, catching the loop before you tighten the stitch. Keeping working on each side of the line in this way until you have covered its length. End off with a small couching stitch that catches the last stitch.

Feather stitch (variation)

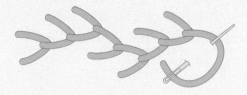

Come up on the left and go in on the right. Come up below that and in the centre, picking up the loop as your tighten the stitch. Working to the right, go into the fabric level where your stitch is at the moment. Come up below that and in the centre, picking up the loop as your tighten the stitch. Now working diagonally to the left, do two more stitches in the same way, after which you will work to the right. Keep working in this way until you have covered the area that you need to and finish off with a small couching stitch that catches the last loop.

Fly stitch

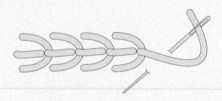

Start at the tip of your shape with a straight stitch. Come up on the left of that stitch, go in at the same level on the right, leaving a loop. Come up in the bottom hole of the straight stitch. Catch the loop and pull through. Make a straight stitch.

French knot

Bring the needle up through the fabric, twist the thread over the needle once or twice and tighten. Go back into the fabric just next to where you came out. Pull the twists that are around the needle down to the bottom. Hold the thread and pull the needle through to form the knot.

French knot – loose

Bring the needle up through the fabric, loosely twist the thread over the needle two or three times. Tighten only slightly and go back into the fabric just next to where you came out. Pull the needle through, controlling the twists as you do so, the aim being to achieve two or three loose loops of thread held down by the thread that goes into the fabric. Working a bunch of these together to fill an area creates the impression of foliage or flowers seen in the distance.

French knot – multiple

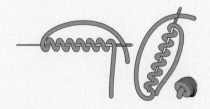

Bring the needle up through the fabric, twist the thread over the needle up to 10 times. Go back into the fabric just next to where you came out, pulling the needle but not all of the thread through. Use the thread that remains on the top of the fabric to tug a few times until all of the loops have tightened into a little ball. Pull the thread through the rest of the way.

Heavy chain stitch

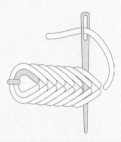

Make a small backstitch at the beginning of the line. Bring the needle up below the backstitch, go under the backstitch and back into where you came out to create a loop. Bring the needle up below the loop you have just made and make another loop through the backstitch. Bring the needle up below the loop you have just made and make a loop through the first loop. Continue by bringing the needle up below the loop just done and making a loop through the second last loop you made.

Interlaced herringbone stitch

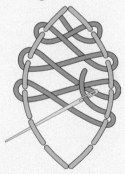

Work a foundation of backstitch on the lines of the shape. Come up under the first backstitch on the left-hand side, go under the second backstitch on the right-hand side. Snake round to go under the first backstitch on the right-hand side and go under second backstitch on the left-hand side. Snake round to go under the first backstitch on the left-hand side and go under the third backstitch on the right-hand side. Keep going in this way until you have filled the shape, going into the fabric under the last backstitch at the bottom.

Knotted cable chain stitch

Working from top to bottom, bring your needle up at the beginning of the line. Make a small stitch under the line, take the working thread over and then under the needle. Pull through, first backwards and then forwards, to tighten the small knot. Pass the needle under the thread before the knot, go into the fabric on the right of the knot and bring your needle up on the line, making sure your thread is under the needle. Pull through to form a loop. Form the next knot by making a small stitch outside the loop and continuing as described above.

Lazy daisy stitch
See Detached Chain Stitch

Long and short stitch

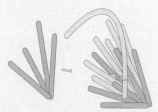

Work with single strand of thread. Starting in the middle of the shape working first to the right and then returning to the middle and working to the left, stitch the darkest colour at the base first. Work straight stitches of random lengths from top to bottom, fanning the stitches so that they favour the centre.

Change to the medium colour thread for the next row, which is started slightly above the darkest colour. Work the stitches going into the fabric between the threads in the previous row. These stitches should also be of random lengths, making them alternately long and short on both ends. Change to the lightest colour for the top row. Following the top outline of the shape, work the third row going into the fabric between the threads in the previous row. These stitches should also be of random lengths, with the ragged edge at the bottom of the row.

Long and short stitch worked with colour variations
If you work long and short stitch in the normal system-atic way when working with multi-coloured thread, you are in danger of ending up with blocks of colour, which are not ideal. The solution to this problem is to spread the colour over the space before it morphs into the next colour.

Starting on one side of the shape – left or right, it doesn't matter – work stitches of varying lengths across the width of the shape, leaving a gap the width of a stitch between them, as depicted above by stitches 1 to 7.

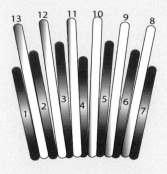

Work back to the side that you started on, filling in the gaps between the stitches with stitches of varying lengths, as depicted above by stitches 8 to 13.

Moving to the next and subsequent rows of stitches, space them in the same way, working from one side to the other with gaps between the stitches, then working back to the first side, filling in those gaps.

Loop stitch

Come up in the middle of the line that you wish to cover. Go in at the top. Come up directly below, on the bottom line, go under the first stitch and over the loop of thread and pull through. Go in at the top. Come up at the bottom and go under the second stitch, over the loop of thread and pull through. Repeat as required. If the rib that is created is not sitting where you would like it to be, it can be moved by adjusting the tension of the stitches.

Outline stitch

It is usually best to do this stitch with one strand of thread. Working from left to right, come up at the beginning of the line. Go in on the line and before pulling the thread through, come up halfway back on the line. Pull through. Go into the fabric halfway further and come up just a little past halfway back, so that you are not coming up in the same hole as where the first stitch finished. Continue to the end of the outline.

Portuguese knotted stem stitch

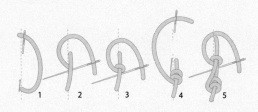

Starting at the beginning of the line, come up through the fabric, go in on the line a little way along and come up on the line halfway back. Pull through. Working backwards towards the beginning of the line, whip the stitch twice. Moving forwards, make another stitch the same length as the first. Come back up at the end of the first stitch. Working backwards again, whip the first half of the present stitch and the last half of the previous stitch together, twice. Repeat as required.

Raised chain stitch

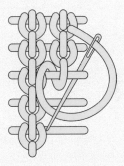

Work a ladder of straight stitch over the area. Come up at the beginning of the ladder in the centre of the first bar. Go over and weave under the bar to the left. Bring the thread around the front and to the right, go under the bar and over the thread. Pull through to form a small knot.

Raised herringbone stitch

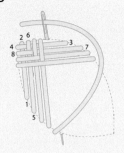

Bring your needle up at 1. Take it back in again at 2. Come up at 3 and go down at 4. Bring it up again at 5 and go into the fabric at 6. Keep going in this way until your shape has been filled. A subtle ridge will form in the centre of the shape.

Raised stem stitch

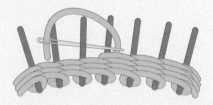

Working from right to left, create a straight stitch ladder which forms the basis of this technique. Working from left to right, bring your needle up slightly past the last straight stitch in the ladder. Go over and under the straight stitches in continuous lines.

Rhodes stitch

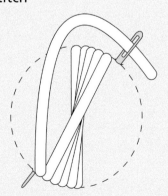

Divide the circle equally by bisecting it with a straight stitch worked from top to bottom. Come up at the top, slightly to the right of the last stitch and go in the bottom, crossing over and going in slightly to the left of the previous stitch. Repeat until you have filled the circle.

Satin stitch

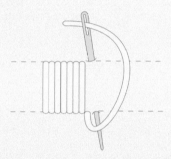

Working from left to right, bring your needle up at the bottom and in at the top, and come out at the bottom again. Place your stitches close together so that no fabric is showing. It is best to work over the shortest side. Stitches can also be placed diagonally or worked from the outside into a central point in the middle.

Sheaf stitch

Consisting of three vertical straight stitches, start with the middle stitch. Place a straight stitch to the right of that stitch. Do a stitch to the left of the middle stitch, but before you tighten it, bring your needle up adjacent to the centre of the middle stitch. Pull through, tightening the left-hand straight stitch. Do a straight stitch over the middle of the three stitches, tucking it under the right-hand stitch, going in adjacent to the middle stitch to pull the three stitches together. You can do a second stitch over the middle if you wish.

Spanish knotted feather stitch

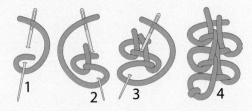

Bring your needle up slightly below and to the right of the beginning of the line. Go in again on and at the beginning of the line. Without pulling through, come up again on the left of the line and catch the loop, making sure that when it tightens it is twisted. Go in on the line below where you went in the last time. Without pulling through, come up again on the right of the line and catch the loop, making sure that when it tightens it is twisted. Using the 3rd and 4th dia-grams above as your guide, continue working twisted loops to the left and right, each time going in on the line below where you went in the last time between the stitches that are above. Finish with a small couch-ing stitch.

Split stitch

Use two strands of thread. Come up at the beginning of the line. Go in again a little way along and before pulling through, come up again in the middle of the stitch, taking your needle up between the two strands of thread. Pull through to tighten.

Stem stitch

Working from left to right, come up just above the line, go in just below the line and come up halfway back, just above the line. Pull through. When using stem stitch as an outline stitch, come up on the line and go in on the line.

Straight stitch

Bring your needle up at the beginning of the stitch and take it into the fabric at the end of the stitch. Stitches can be of equal or unequal length, or as directed in the instructions in your embroidery pattern.

Trellis couching – basic

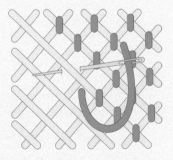

Work a layer of long straight stitches across the area. These can be vertical or diagonal. Work another layer of long straight stitches that are placed at right angles to the first layer. Work small, straight couching stitches over the intersection of the stitches.

Trellis – cross-stitch couching

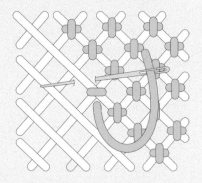

Variation 1: Work a layer of diagonal long straight stitches across the area. Work another layer of long straight stitches that are placed at right angles to the first layer. Work small cross stitches over the intersection of the stitches.

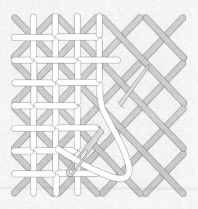

Variation 2: To create an interesting basket weave effect, start each leg of the cross-stitch couching in the middle of the block of space between the trellis stitches, ending in the middle of the opposite block. Make the stitches go in and out of the same holes.

Trellis couching – cross-stitch filling

Using thread shade 1, work a layer of pairs of long straight stitches across the area. These can be horizontal or diagonal. Work another layer of pairs of long straight stitches that are placed at right angles to the first layer. Using thread shade 2, work small, straight couching stitches over each thread of the Intersections. Work from the outside into the middle of each intersection, each stitch going into the same hole.

Trellis couching – woven

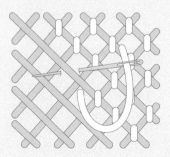

Using thread shade 1, work a layer of long straight stitches across the area. These can be horizontal or diagonal. Work another layer of long straight stitches that are placed at right angles to the first layer. Using thread shade 2, work small, straight couching stitches over the intersection of the long stitches.

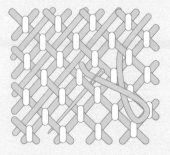

Using thread shade 3, weave over and under the shade 1 lines.

Using thread shade 4, and working at right angles, weave under the first of layer of trellis (shade 1 stitches) and over the weaving that you have just done (shade 3).

Tufting (bad hair day)

Bring the needle up through the fabric and go down again just next to where you came out. When pulling through, leave a loop. Come up on the right of the spot you went in, working backwards, and do a backstitch over the bottom ends of the loop. This locks the loop into place and causes it to lie away from the direction of stitching. Working forwards again, come up just past the beginning of the backstitch to start the next loop. Keep making loops of varying lengths until you have filled the area – how many loops you make will depend on how much you need to fill the area; generally it would be less than you would need for fluffy tufting (below) as you would want the effect to be somewhat 'moth eaten'. When you have ended off the thread, snip each loop individually and cut the strands to the lengths (usually variable) that you require.

Tufting (fluffy)

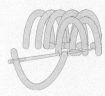

Bring the needle up through the fabric and go down again a few millimetres away. When pulling through, leave a loop. Come up to the left of the spot you went in – about halfway back – and go back in through the same hole that you went into at the end of the loop. Pull through to form a backstitch. This locks the loop. Bring the needle up half way back – just before the beginning of the backstitch and form the next loop by going halfway further, completing that loop with a backstitch. Fill the area you wish to cover with rows of loop/backstitch combinations working in both directions. When you have ended off the thread, give the loops a haircut with a sharp pair of scissors. Cut as short as you can as this gives a fluffier appearance. The stitches around the edge should be shorter than those in the middle.

Up and down buttonhole stitch

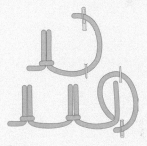

Working from left to right, bring the needle up on the bottom edge where you require the ridge. Take the needle in at the top edge, and out again at the bottom edge, with the thread looped under the needle. Pull through. Go over the thread, insert the needle on the line, bringing it up again adjacent to the upper part of the stitch, as depicted. Making sure that the thread is looped under the needle, pull upwards and then downwards to continue.

Vermicelli couching

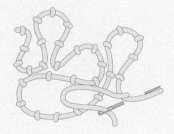

Thread a needle with two strands of thread and another with a single strand of thread. Come through the fabric with the two-strand needle and couch that thread into a series of rounded squiggles that move all over the area that you wish to cover, but never cross over each other. At the edges of the section go into the fabric and come up again further along continuing the pattern.

Vermicelli couching – two-thread

To work a two-thread variation, follow the instructions for vermicelli couching above, working with two strands of cotton couched down with a single strand. Make sure that the swirls are large enough to accommodate a second sequence of swirls. The second sequence requires that a single strand is couched with a single strand, swirling in between the existing couching on both sides of each line.

Wheatear stitch

Working from top to bottom, work a detached chain, starting just below and stretching to the beginning. Place a diagonal straight stitch on each side of this stitch. Come up slightly below, and work a loop through all the threads of the straight and detached chain stitches. Place a diagonal straight stitch on each side of this loop. Repeat as required.

Whipped backstitch

To whip backstitch, bring your needle up adjacent to the beginning of the line of stitching. Take your needle and thread over, then under each stitch. It is advisable to use a tapestry needle when whipping. A contrasting colour thread is often effective.

Whipped stem stitch

To whip stem stitch, bring your needle up adjacent to the beginning of the line of stem stitch. Take your needle and thread over, then under the section where that stitch and the next stitch lie adjacent to each other. It is advisable to use a tapestry needle when whipping. A contrasting colour thread is often effective.

Woven raised chain stitch

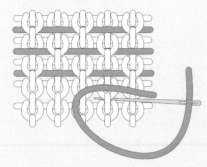

Work long horizontal stitches over the area that you want to fill, making these stitches 3 mm apart. Using the same thread, work vertical raised chain (described above in alphabetical sequence) which is attached to the long horizontal stitches. With a contrasting thread on a tapestry needle, weave over and under the threads that run between the raised chain knots, alternating the sequence in each row so that where you have gone over a thread in a row, you will go under it in the next row. Take your needle into the fabric at the end of each row, coming up at the beginning for the next row.

Working with twisted thread

The easiest way to convert stranded cotton into cord with which to embroider is to acquire a Spinster tool. It is, however, possible to twist it by turning it between your index finger and thumb, or to place a pencil in the loop and turn that.

- Cut a strand length of thread that measures about 2 m (2.2 yd).
- Fold it double and tie the two ends together with an overhand knot.
- Loop one end over something that won't move, like a cup-hook or a doorknob.
- Loop the other end over the hook on the Spinster and pull the yarn taut.

- Now wind the threads until they are firmly twisted together. Test from time to time by relaxing the tension and allowing the threads to twist around each other. When you are happy with the twist, double the twisted thread over by placing the two ends together.

- Hang the Spinster, or something heavy, at the fold to add weight so that it will twist together evenly.
- Pull all the threads off the cup hook.
- Holding the ends together, allow the thread to hang from your fingers and twist freely.
- Once they stop twisting, do an overhand knot at the raw ends to keep them together. Snip off the raw ends after the knot for the sake of neatness.
- Use the cord in a needle with a large eye, such as a size 20 tapestry or chenille needle.

Bead embroidery techniques

THREE-DIMENSIONAL BEADED ELEMENTS: GENERAL INSTRUCTIONS

ABBREVIATIONS:
PU: Pick up
GT: Go through
GU: Go up
GD: Go down

- Use a size 12 beading needle or a size 11 sharps quilting needle.
- Use fine beading thread as recommended in each pattern.
- Because you are attaching the beaded items to fabric, it is vital to check that the thread is colour-fast:
  > Wind a small amount onto a plastic floss card;
  > Plunge the card into very hot – almost boiling – water;
  > Remove it and pat it dry on a light coloured towel;
  > If there is no colour left on the towel, it is safe to use.
- It is important to note that when working each component of these objects, your stitching tension should be extremely tight. If it is not tight, the elements will be floppy which is not ideal.

To start
To start these bead items, PU 1 bead. GT it a second time without snagging the thread. Pull it down towards the end of the thread, leaving a tail of approximately 15 cm (6"). This will act as a stopper bead and you will remove it eventually.

Accommodating bead size variations
In each petal that you do, you need to go through bead no. 1 a few times and when you are using size 15° beads, there is a danger that it will become clogged up with thread. Where relevant, two diagrams and their instructions are provided.

Changing thread
- Try to work the entire element with a continuous strand of thread, up to 1½ metres (1⅔ yards).
- This may not be possible with some of the larger flowers. If you need to start a new thread, try to finish off at the completion of a petal, starting a new thread with a new petal.

TO END THE THREAD:
1. Work the needle and thread to the top of the petal or leaf.
2. Work a half hitch over the thread that runs between the bead you have come out of and the bead next to it, as under.

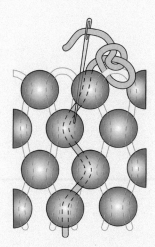

3. Take the needle over the thread, then under it. Continue by going over and under the working thread.

4. Pull tight to form a knot over the interleading thread.

5. Take the needle back down the bead you came out of.

6. Pull tight until you feel the knot click into the bead. This will pull the knot back and make it invisible.

7. Work down a few beads, bringing the needle out on the wrong side and snip off the thread.

TO START A NEW THREAD:

1. Work up a few beads with the new thread coming out of a different bead close to where you ended off.

2. Make a half hitch over the interleading thread.

3. Having pulled the knot into the bead you came out of, work down the beads of the petal until you exit the bead at the bottom.

4. Continue adding beads according to the pattern.

Joining petals to complete beaded flowers

In the final stages of the fifth petal of the flower, you will need to join the side of that petal to corresponding beads on the side of the first petal with square stitch. The number of beads you join will depend on how many beads have been joined in the construction of the flower, varying from two to four and even more if the flower is large. The general instructions below relate to the 10-bead flower.

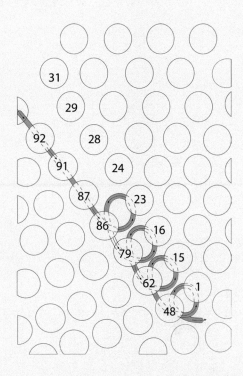

Referring to the diagram above, in the final stages of the last petal:

1. GD beads 92 to 86 (the 4th bead from the bottom) of the last petal

2. GU bead 23 (the 4th bead from the bottom) of the first petal

3. GD beads 86 and 79 of the last petal

4. GU bead 16 of the first petal

5. GD beads 79 and 62 of the last petal

6. GU bead 15 of the first petal

7. GD beads 62 and 48 of the last petal

8. GU bead 1 of the first petal

9. GD bead 48 of the last petal

You have been working on the wrong side of the petal. This is why you can see many of the threads that run up the side of the beads. Turn your flower over and these working threads will not be visible.

Attaching flowers and leaves to the fabric

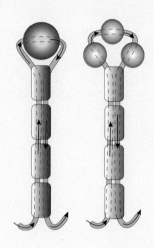

The diagram above depicts the centre of the flower.

- There should be two tails of thread at the base of the completed flower. Thread the longest tail on a beading needle.
- Take the needle through the fabric at the point where you would like to place the flower.
- Bring the needle up in the small gap in the centre of the flower at approximately the place where two petals abut each other.
- Work a small couching stitch over the thread, or threads, that run from the bottom bead of the one petal to the bottom bead of the adjacent petal.
- Work the same stitch over the threads at the meeting points of the remaining petals.
- Come up through the fabric behind one of the petals approximately level with the second or third bead up from the base of the flower.
- Take the needle through the closest bead and back into the fabric.
- Attach a second petal through a bead, at the back, on the opposite side of the flower.
- If you have sufficient thread left on the needle, come up in the centre of the flower. (If not, end off that thread and use the remaining tail.)
- Pick up as many beads as you need to make a stamen in the centre of the flower. Consider a different, often larger bead at the top.

- Change direction, bringing the needle back down all the beads, except for the top one that acts as a stopper bead.
- Go back into the fabric and either end off or come back up a few more times to make additional stamens as needed.
- Once you have your flowers in place, arrange the leaves where you would like them to be, using the same method.
- There should be two tails of thread at the base of the completed leaf. Thread the longest tail on a beading needle.

- Take the needle through the fabric at the point where you would like to place the leaf, tucking the bottom end under the petal of a flower.
- Come up through the fabric adjacent to the second or third bead on one side of the leaf.
- Take the needle through that bead and back into the fabric.
- End off that thread and do the same with the second thread, attaching a bead on the opposite side of the leaf.
- When you have placed all the leaves, complete the arrangement of flowers by placing twigs and small branches around the flowers and leaves.
- These are worked in the same way as the stamens using small beads for the stalk and larger beads for the tip.
- Bring the needle up through the fabric from underneath the petals of the flowers so that these twigs radiate from the flowers. Make a variety of lengths.
- If the twigs won't lie the way you want them to, place a small couching stitch between two of the beads in the stalk, two or three beads up from the base.

FLOWERS

Four-bead flower

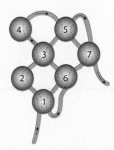

Diagram 1

Referring to diagram 1 above and working with 1,5 m (1²/₃ yd) of thread:

1. PU beads 1 to 5

2. GD bead 3

3. PU bead 6

4. GD bead 1

5. GU bead 6

6. PU bead 7

7. GU bead 5

8. GD bead 7

Diagram 2.1 (for size 11° beads)

Referring to diagram 2.1 above (if you are using size 15° beads refer to diagram 2.2 on page 36), turn your work over and work down beads 6 and 1, exiting the bottom bead.

1. #GU bead 2

2. PU bead 8

3. GU bead 4

4. GD bead 8#

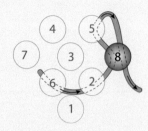

Diagram 2.2 (for size 15° beads)

Referring to diagram 2.2 above, turn your work over. GD bead 6 and then follow the instructions from # to # in diagram 2.1 on page 35.

SECOND PETAL:

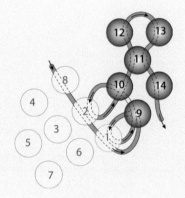

Diagram 3

Referring to diagram 3 above, add the second petal:
1. GD beads 2 and 1
2. PU bead 9
3. GD bead 1 and GU bead 9
4. PU bead 10
5. GD bead 2 and GU bead 10
6. PU beads 11, 12 and 13
7. GD bead 11
8. PU bead 14 and GD bead 9

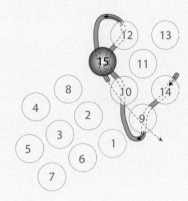

Diagram 4.1 (for size 11° beads)

1. #GU bead 10
2. PU bead 15 and GU bead 12
3. GD bead 15#
4. Continue down beads 10 and 9 to the bottom

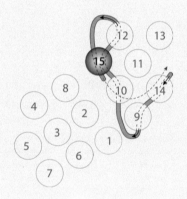

Diagram 4.2 (for size 15° beads)

1. Follow the instructions from # to # in diagram 4.1 above
2. Continue down bead 10
3. GU bead 14

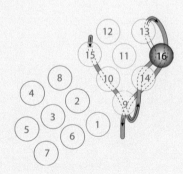

Diagram 5.1 (for size 11° beads)

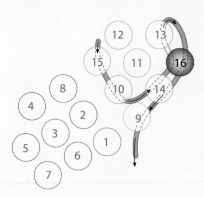

Diagram 5.2 (for size 15° beads)

Referring to diagram 5.1 on page 26 for size 11° beads or 5.2 above for size 15° beads:
1. GU bead 14
2. PU bead 16 and GU bead 13
3. GD beads 16, 14 and 9

Following the instructions for the second petal, continue adding petals until you have completed the fifth petal. In the final stages of the last petal and following the instructions for completing the flower in the general knowledge at the beginning of this gallery, work down the side of the last petal joining the two beads at the bottom.

Six-bead flower

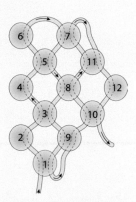

Diagram 1

Referring to diagram 1 above and working with 1,5m (1²⁄₃ yd) of thread:
1. PU beads 1 to 7
2. GD bead 5, PU bead 8
3. GD bead 3, PU bead 9
4. GD bead 1
5. GU bead 9
6. PU bead 10, GU bead 8
7. PU bead 11, GU bead 7
8. GD bead 11
9. PU bead 12, GD bead 10

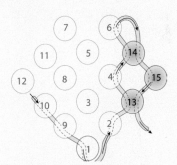

Diagram 2.1 (for size 11° beads)

Referring to diagram 2.1 above, turn your work over and work down beads 10, 9 and 1, exiting the bottom bead.
1. #GU bead 2
2. PU bead 13, GU bead 4
3. PU bead 14, GU bead 6
4. GD bead 14
5. PU bead 15, GD bead 13#

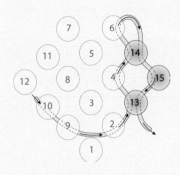

Diagram 2.2 (for size 15° beads)

Turn your work over and work down bead 9. Follow the instructions from # to # in diagram 2.1 on page 37.

SECOND PETAL:

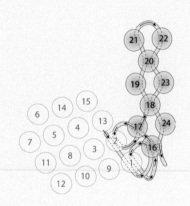

Diagram 3

Referring to diagram 3 above, add the second petal:

1. GD beads 15, 13, 2 and 1
2. PU bead 16
3. GD bead 1 and GU bead 16
4. PU bead 17
5. GD bead 2, GU bead 17
6. PU beads 18 to 22
7. GD bead 20
8. PU bead 23 and GD bead 18
9. PU bead 24 and GD bead 16

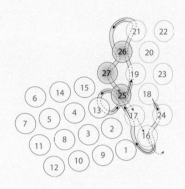

Diagram 4.1 (for size 11° beads)

1. #GU bead 17
2. PU bead 25 and GD bead 13
3. GU bead 25 and bead 19
4. PU bead 26, GU bead 21, GD bead 26
5. PU bead 27 and GD bead 25#
6. Following the pink arrow, keep going down the side of the petal by GD beads 17 and 16, exiting at the bottom of the petal

Diagram 4.2 (for size 15° beads)

1. Follow the instructions from # to # in diagram 2.1 on page 37
2. Following the pink arrow, GD bead 17
3. GU bead 24

Diagram 5.1 (for size 11° beads)

Refer to diagram 5.1 or 5.2:

1. GU bead 24

2. PU bead 28 and GU bead 23

3. PU bead 29 and GU bead 22

4. GD bead 29

5. PU bead 30 and GD beads 28, 24 and 16

Diagram 5.2 (for size 15° beads)

Following the instructions for the second petal, continue adding petals until you have completed the fifth petal. In the final stages of the last petal and following the general instructions on page 33 for completing the flower, work down the side of the last petal joining the two beads at the bottom.

Eight-bead flower

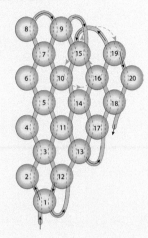

Diagram 1

Referring to diagram 1 above and working with 1,5 m (1²⁄₃ yd) of thread:

1. PU beads 1 to 9

2. GD bead 7, PU bead 10

3. GD bead 5, PU bead 11

4. GD bead 3, PU bead 12

5. GD bead 1

6. GU bead 12

7. PU bead 13, GU bead 11

8. PU bead 14, GU bead 10

9. PU bead 15, GU bead 9

10. GD bead 15

11. PU bead 16, GD bead 14

12. PU bead 17, GD bead 13

13. GU bead 17

14. PU bead 18, GU bead 16

15. PU bead 19

16. Working backwards towards the centre GD beads 15 and 10

17. GU beads 16 and 15

18. GD bead 19

19. PU bead 20, GD bead 18

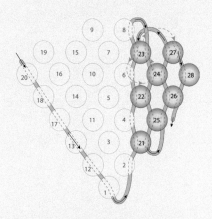

Diagram 2.1 (for size 11° beads)

Referring to diagram 2.1 above, turn your work over and work down bead 17 to 1, exiting at the bottom of the petal.

1. #GU bead 2
2. PU bead 21, GU bead 4
3. PU bead 22, GU bead 6
4. PU bead 23, GU bead 8
5. GD bead 23
6. PU bead 24, GD bead 22
7. PU bead 25, GD bead 21
8. GU bead 25
9. PU bead 26, GU bead 24
10. PU bead 27
11. Working backwards towards the centre, GD beads 23 and 6
12. GU beads 24 and 23
13. GD bead 27
14. PU bead 28, GD bead 26#

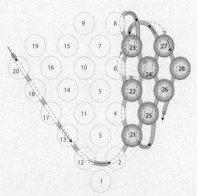

Diagram 2.2 (for size 15° beads)

Referring to diagram 2.2 above, turn your work over and work down bead beads 17, 13 and 12. Follow the instructions from # to # in diagram 2.1 on the left.

SECOND PETAL:

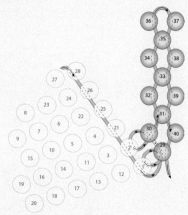

Diagram 3

Referring to diagram 3 above, add the second petal:

1. GD beads 25, 21, 2 and 1
2. PU bead 29
3. GD bead 1 and GU bead 29
4. PU bead 30
5. GD bead 2, GU bead 30
6. PU beads 31 to 37
7. GD bead 35
8. PU bead 38 and GD bead 33
9. PU bead 39 and GD bead 31
10. PU bead 40 and GD bead 29

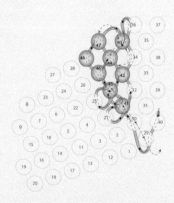

Diagram 4.1 (for size 11° beads)

Referring to diagram 4.1 above:

1. #GU bead 30

2. PU bead 41 and GD bead 21

3. GU bead 41 and bead 32

4. PU bead 42, GU bead 34

5. PU bead 43, GU bead 36

6. GD bead 43

7. PU bead 44 and GD bead 42

8. PU bead 45 and GU bead 25

9. GD bead 45 and bead 41

10. GU bead 45

11. PU bead 46 and GU bead 44

12. PU bead 47

13. Working backwards towards the centre, GD beads 43 and 34

14. GU beads 44 and 43

15. GD bead 47

16. PU bead 48 and GD bead 46#

17. Following the pink arrow, go down the side of the petal through beads 45 to 29

18. GU bead 40

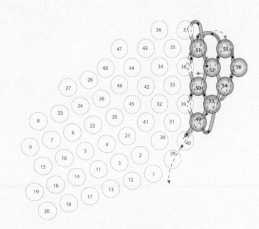

Diagram 5

Refer to diagram 5 above:

1. PU bead 49 and GU bead 39

2. PU bead 50 and GU bead 38

3. PU bead 51 and GU bead 37

4. GD bead 51

5. PU bead 52 and GD bead 50

6. PU bead 53 and GD bead 49

7. GU bead 53

8. PU bead 54 and GU bead 52

9. PU bead 55

10. Working backwards towards the centre, GD beads 51 and 38

11. GU beads 52 and 51

12. GD bead 55

13. PU bead 56 and GD bead 54

14. Following the pink arrow, go down the side of the petal through beads 53 to 29, exiting at the bottom of the petal

Following the instructions for the second petal, continue adding petals until you have completed the fifth petal. In the final stages of the last petal and following the general instructions on page 33 for completing the flower, work down the side of the last petal joining the two beads at the bottom.

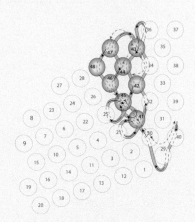

Diagram 4.2 (for size 15° beads)

Referring to diagram 4.2 above:

1. Follow the instructions from # to # in diagram 4.1 on page 40

2. Following the pink arrow, go down the side of the petal through beads 45 to 29

3. GU bead 40

Ten-bead flower

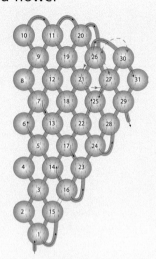

Diagram 1

Referring to diagram 1 above and working with 1,5 m (1²⁄₃ yd) of thread:
1. PU beads 1 to 11, GD bead 9
2. PU bead 12, GD bead 7
3. PU bead 13, GD bead 5
4. PU bead 14, GD bead 3
5. PU bead 15, GD bead 1
6. GU bead 15
7. PU bead 16, GU bead 14
8. PU bead 17, GU bead 13
9. PU bead 18, GU bead 12
10. PU bead 19, GU bead 11
11. PU bead 20, GD bead 19
12. PU bead 21, GD bead 18
13. PU bead 22, GD bead 17
14. PU bead 23, GD bead 16
15. GU bead 23
16. PU bead 24, GU bead 22
17. PU bead 25, GU bead 21
18. PU bead 26, GU bead 20
19. GD bead 26
20. PU bead 27, GD bead 25
21. PU bead 28, GD bead 24
22. GU bead 28
23. PU bead 29, GU bead 27
24. PU bead 30

25. Working backwards towards the centre, GD beads 26 and 21
26. GU beads 27 and 26
27. GD bead 30
28. PU bead 31, GD bead 29

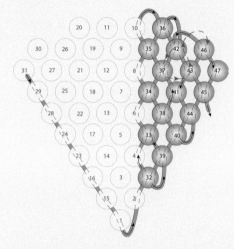

Diagram 2.1 (for size 11° or Delica beads)

Referring to diagram 2.1 above (if you are using size 15° beads refer to diagram 2.2 on page 43), turn your work over and work down beads 29 to 1, exiting the bottom bead.
1. #GU bead 2
2. PU bead 32, GU bead 4
3. PU bead 33, GU bead 6
4. PU bead 34, GU bead 8
5. PU bead 35, GU bead 10
6. PU bead 36, GD bead 35
7. PU bead 37, GD bead 34
8. PU bead 38, GD bead 33
9. PU bead 39, GD bead 32
10. GU bead 39
11. PU bead 40, GU bead 38
12. PU bead 41, GU bead 37
13. PU bead 42, GU bead 36
14. GD bead 42
15. PU bead 43, GD bead 41
16. PU bead 44, GD bead 40
17. GU bead 44
18. PU bead 45, GU bead 43
19. PU bead 46

20. Working backwards towards the centre, GD beads 42 and 37

21. GU beads 43 and 42

22. GD bead 46

23. PU bead 47, GD bead 45#

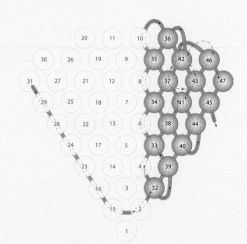

Diagram 2.2 (for size 15° beads)

Referring to diagram 2.2 above, turn your work over and work down beads 29 to 15. Thereafter, GU bead 2 and follow the instructions from # to # as described for 2.1 on page 42.

SECOND PETAL:

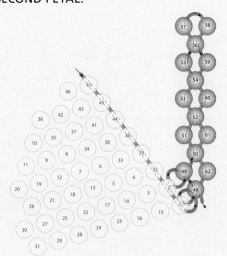

Diagram 3

Referring to diagram 3 below left, add the second petal:

1. GD beads 45 to 1, exiting at the bottom bead

2. PU bead 48

3. GD bead 1 and GU bead 48

4. PU bead 49

5. GD bead 2, GU bead 49

6. PU beads 50 to 58

7. GD bead 56

8. PU bead 59 and GD bead 54

9. PU bead 60 and GD bead 52

10. PU bead 61 and GD bead 50

11. PU bead 62 and GD bead 48

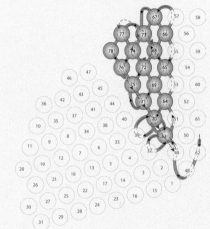

Diagram 4

Referring to diagram 4:

1. GU bead 49

2. PU bead 63 and GD bead 32

3. GU bead 63 and bead 51

4. PU bead 64, GU bead 53

5. PU bead 65, GU bead 55

6. PU bead 66, GU bead 57

7. PU bead 67, GD bead 66

8. PU bead 68, GD bead 65

9. PU bead 69, GD bead 64

10. PU bead 70, GU bead 39

11. GD bead 70 and bead 63

12. GU bead 70

13. PU bead 71, GU bead 69

14. PU bead 72, GU bead 68

15. PU bead 73, GU bead 67

16. GD bead 73

17. PU bead 74, GD bead 72

18. PU bead 75, GD bead 71

19. GU bead 75

20. PU bead 76, GU bead 74

21. PU bead 77

22. Working backwards towards the centre, GD beads 73 and 68

23. GU beads 74 and 73

24. GD bead 77

25. PU bead 78 and GD bead 76

26. Following the pink arrow, keep going down the side of the petals through beads 75 to 49

14. GD bead 89

15. PU bead 90, GD bead 88

16. PU bead 91, GD bead 87

17. GU bead 91

18. PU bead 92, GU bead 90

19. PU bead 93

20. Working backwards towards the centre GD beads 89 and 84

21. GU beads 90 and 89

22. GD bead 93

23. PU bead 94, GD bead 92

24. Following the pink arrow, keep going down the side of the petal by GD beads 91 to 48, exiting at the bottom of the petal#

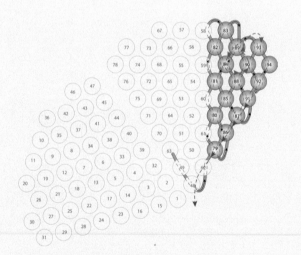

Diagram 5.1 (for size 11° or Delica beads)

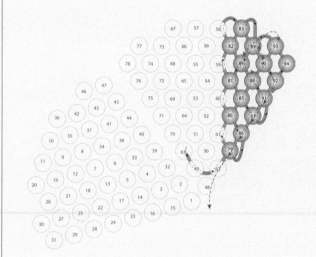

Diagram 5.2 (for size 15° beads)

Referring to diagram 5.1 above:

1. GD bead 48, GU bead 62

2. #PU bead 79, GU bead 61

3. PU bead 80, GU bead 60

4. PU bead 81, GU bead 59

5. PU bead 82, GU bead 58

6. PU bead 83, GD bead 82

7. PU bead 84, GD bead 81

8. PU bead 85, GD bead 80

9. PU bead 86, GD bead 79

10. GU bead 86

11. PU bead 87, GU bead 85

12. PU bead 88, GU bead 84

13. PU bead 89, GU bead 83

Referring to diagram 5.2 above:

1. GD bead 49, GU bead 62

2. Follow the instructions from # to # as described for diagram 5.1 left.

Following the instructions for the second petal, continue adding petals until you have completed the fifth petal. In the final stages of the last petal and following the general instructions on page 33 for completing the flower, work down the side of the last petal joining the four beads at the bottom.

Twelve-bead flower

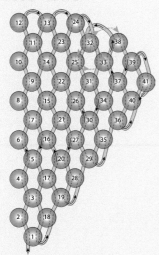

Diagram 1

Referring to diagram 1 above and working with 1,5 m (1²⁄₃ yd) of thread:

1. PU beads 1 to 13, GD bead 11

2. PU bead 14, GD bead 9

3. PU bead 15, GD bead 7

4. PU bead 16, GD bead 5

5. PU bead 17, GD bead 3

6. PU bead 18, GD bead 1

7. GU bead 18

8. PU bead 19, GU bead 17

9. PU bead 20, GU bead 16

10. PU bead 21, GU bead 15

11. PU bead 22, GU bead 14

12. PU bead 23, GU bead 13

13. PU bead 24, GD bead 23

14. PU bead 25, GD bead 22

15. PU bead 26, GD bead 21

16. PU bead 27, GD bead 20

17. PU bead 28, GD bead 19

18. GU bead 28

19. PU bead 29, GU bead 27

20. PU bead 30, GU bead 26

21. PU bead 31, GU bead 25

22. PU bead 32, GU bead 24

23. GD bead 32

24. PU bead 33, GD bead 31

25. PU bead 35, GD bead 30

26. PU bead 35, GD bead 29

27. GU bead 35

28. PU bead 36, GU bead 34

29. PU bead 37, GU bead 33

30. PU bead 38

31. Working backwards towards the centre GD beads 32 and 25

32. GU beads 33 and 32

33. GD bead 38

34. PU bead 39, GD bead 37

35. PU bead 40, GD bead 36

36. GU bead 40

37. PU bead 41, GU bead 39

38. GD bead 41

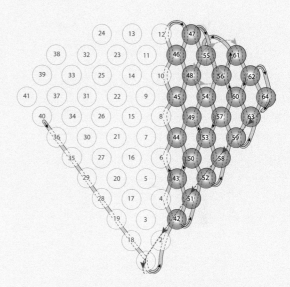

Diagram 2.1 (for size 11° or Delica beads)

Referring to diagram 2.1 above (if you are using size 15° beads refer to diagram 2.2 on page 46), turn your work over and work down beads 40 to 1, exiting the bottom bead.

1. GU bead 2

2. #PU bead 42, GU bead 4

3. PU bead 43, GU bead 6

4. PU bead 44, GU bead 8

5. PU bead 45, GU bead 10

6. PU bead 46, GU bead 12

7. PU bead 47, GD bead 46

8. PU bead 48, GD bead 45

9. PU bead 49, GD bead 44
10. PU bead 50, GD bead 43
11. PU bead 51, GD bead 42
12. GU bead 51
13. PU bead 52, GU bead 50
14. PU bead 53, GU bead 49
15. PU bead 54, GU bead 48
16. PU bead 55, GU bead 47
17. GD bead 55
18. PU bead 56, GD bead 54
19. PU bead 57, GD bead 53
20. PU bead 58, GD bead 52
21. GU bead 58
22. PU bead 59, GU bead 57
23. PU bead 60, GU bead 56
24. PU bead 61
25. Working backwards towards the centre, GD beads 55 and 48
26. GU beads 56 and 55
27. GD bead 61
28. PU bead 62, GD bead 60
29. PU bead 63, GD bead 59
30. GU bead 63
31. PU bead 64, GU bead 62
32. GD bead 64 and following the pink arrow in the diagram continue down beads 63 to 1, exiting at the bottom#

In each petal that you do, you need to go through bead no. 1 a few times and when you are using size 15° beads, there is a danger that it will become clogged up with thread. Avoid going through bead no. 1 in this step as described below:

Referring to diagram 2.2 below left, turn your work over and work down beads 40 to 18. Thereafter, GU bead 2 and follow the instructions from # to # as described for 2.1 on page 45.

SECOND PETAL:

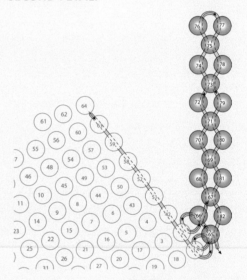

Diagram 3

Referring to diagram 3 above, add the second petal:
1. GD beads 63 to 1, exiting at the bottom bead
2. PU bead 65
3. GD bead 1 and GU bead 65
4. PU bead 66
5. GD bead 2, GU bead 66
6. PU beads 67 to 77
7. GD bead 75
8. PU bead 78 and GD bead 73
9. PU bead 79 and GD bead 71
10. PU bead 80 and GD bead 69
11. PU bead 81 and GD bead 67
12. PU bead 82 and GD bead 65

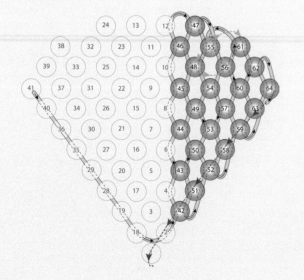

Diagram 2.2 (for size 15° beads)

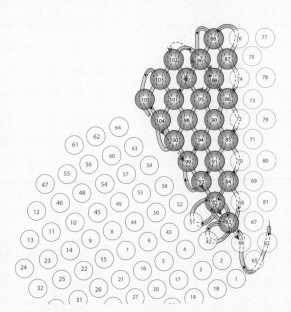

Diagram 4

Referring to diagram 4:

1. GU bead 66

2. PU bead 83 and GD bead 42

3. GU bead 83 and bead 68

4. PU bead 84, GU bead 70

5. PU bead 85, GU bead 72

6. PU bead 86, GU bead 74

7. PU bead 87, GU bead 76

8. PU bead 88, GD bead 87

9. PU bead 89, GD bead 86

10. PU bead 90, GD bead 85

11. PU bead 91, GU bead 84

12. PU bead 92

13. GU bead 51, GD bead 92 and 83

14. GU bead 92

15. PU bead 93, GU bead 91

16. PU bead 94, GU bead 90

17. PU bead 95, GU bead 89

18. PU bead 96, GU bead 88

19. GD bead 96

20. PU bead 97, GD bead 95

21. PU bead 98, GD bead 94

22. PU bead 99, GD bead 93

23. GU bead 99

24. PU bead 100, GU bead 98

25. PU bead 101, GU bead 97

26. PU bead 102

27. Working backwards towards the centre, GD beads 96 and 89

28. GU beads 97 and 96

29. GD bead 102

30. PU bead 103, GD bead 101

31. PU bead 104, GD bead 100

32. GU bead 104

33. PU bead 105, GU bead 103

34. GD bead 105

35. Following the pink arrow, keep going down the side of the petals through beads 104 to 66

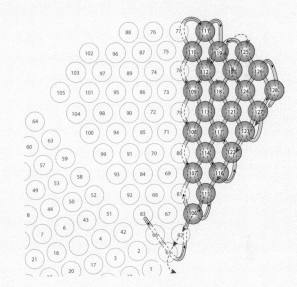

Diagram 5.1 (for size 11° or Delica beads)

Referring to diagram 5.1 above:

1. GD bead 65, exiting at the bottom

2. GU bead 82

3. #PU bead 106, GU bead 81

4. PU bead 107, GU bead 80

5. PU bead 108, GU bead 79

6. PU bead 109, GU bead 78

7. PU bead 110, GU bead 77

8. PU bead 111, GD bead 110

9. PU bead 112, GD bead 109

10. PU bead 113, GD bead 108

11. PU bead 114, GD bead 107

12. PU bead 115, GD bead 106

13. GU bead 115

14. PU bead 116, GU bead 114

15. PU bead 117, GU bead 113

16. PU bead 118, GU bead 112

17. PU bead 119, GU bead 111

18. GD bead 119

19. PU bead 120, GD bead 118

20. PU bead 121, GD bead 117

21. PU bead 122, GD bead 116

22. GU bead 122

23. PU bead 123, GU bead 121

24. PU bead 124, GU bead 120

25. PU bead 125

26. Working backwards towards the centre, GD beads 119 and 112

27. GU beads 120 and 119

28. GD bead 125

29. PU bead 126, GD bead 124

30. PU bead 127, GD bead 123

31. GU bead 127

32. PU bead 128, GU bead 126

33. GD bead 128

34. Following the pink arrow, keep going down the side of the petal through beads 127 to 65, exiting at the bottom of the petal#

Referring to diagram 5.2 below left:

1. GU bead 82

2. Follow the instructions from # to # as described for diagram 2.1 on page 45.

Following the instructions for the second petal, continue adding petals until you have completed the fifth petal. In the final stages of the last petal and following the general instructions on page 33 for completing the flower, work down the side of the last petal, joining the four beads at the bottom.

Beaded 'orchid'

In Roger the Rhino 10-, 12- and 14-bead orchids are used. This generic pattern picks up 12 beads in the first row of the petal. Adjust the size of the flower by picking up 10, 12 or 14 beads in the first row. Depending on the number of beads in that first row, you will do more or fewer rows, always being aware that your last row on each side should consist of two beads with a gap between them.

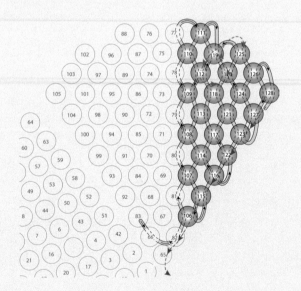

Diagram 5.2 (for size 15° beads)

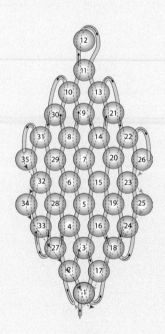

Diagram 1

Referring to diagram 1 above and working with 1,5 m (1²⁄₃ yd) of thread:

1. PU beads 1 to 12, GD bead 11

2. PU bead 13, GD bead 9

3. PU bead 14, GD bead 7

4. PU bead 15, GD bead 5

5. PU bead 16, GD bead 3

6. PU bead 17, GD bead 1

7. GU bead 17

8. PU bead 18, GU bead 16

9. PU bead 19, GU bead 15

10. PU bead 20, GU bead 14

11. PU bead 21, GU bead 13

12. GD bead 21

13. PU bead 22, GD bead 20

14. PU bead 23, GD bead 19

15. PU bead 24, GD bead 18

16. GU bead 24

17. PU bead 25, GU bead 23

18. PU bead 26, GU bead 22

19. GD bead 26

20. Following the green arrow, keep going down the side of the petal through beads 23 down to 1

21. GU bead 2

22. PU bead 27, GU bead 4

23. PU bead 28, GU bead 6

24. PU bead 29, GU bead 8

25. PU bead 30, GU bead 10

26. GD bead 30

27. PU bead 31, GD bead 29

28. PU bead 32, GD bead 28

29. PU bead 33, GD bead 27

30. GU bead 33

31. PU bead 34, GU bead 32

32. PU bead 35, GU bead 31

33. GD bead 35

34. Following the red arrow, keep going down the side of the petal through beads 32 down to 1, exiting at the bottom of the petal

SECOND PETAL

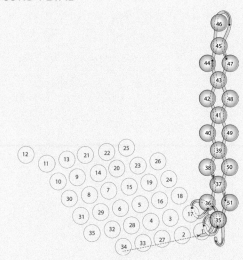

Diagram 2

Referring to diagram 2 above, add the second petal.

1. PU bead 35

2. GD bead 1, GU bead 35

3. PU bead 36

4. GD bead 17, GU bead 36

5. PU beads 37 to 46

6. GD bead 45

7. PU bead 47, GD bead 43

8. PU bead 48, GD bead 41

9. PU bead 49, GD bead 39

10. PU bead 50, GD bead 37

11. PU bead 51, GD bead 35

12. GU bead 36

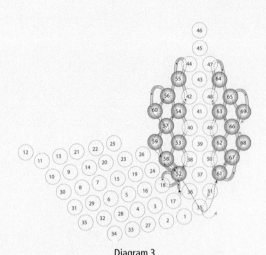

Diagram 3

Referring to diagram 3 above and starting at the spot indicated by the short purple arrow, complete the second petal.

1. PU bead 52

2. GD bead 18, GU bead 52 and bead 38

3. PU bead 53, GU bead 40

4. PU bead 54, GU bead 42

5. PU bead 55, GU bead 44

6. GD bead 55

7. PU bead 56, GD bead 54

8. PU bead 57, GD bead 53

9. PU bead 58, GD bead 52

10. GU bead 58

11. PU bead 59, GU bead 57

12. PU bead 60, GU bead 56

13. GD bead 60

14. Following the red arrow, keep going down the side of the petal through beads 57 down to 35 exiting at the bottom of the petal

15. GU bead 51

16. PU bead 61, GU bead 50

17. PU bead 62, GU bead 49

18. PU bead 63, GU bead 48

19. PU bead 64, GU bead 47

20. GD bead 64

21. PU bead 65, GD bead 63

22. PU bead 66, GD bead 62

23. PU bead 67, GD bead 61

24. GU bead 67

25. PU bead 68, GU bead 66

26. PU bead 69, GU bead 65

27. GD bead 69

28. Following the green arrow, keep going down the side of the petal through beads 66 down to 35 exiting at the bottom of the petal

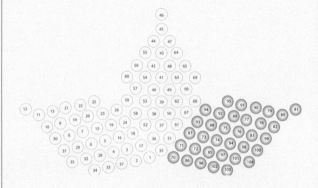

Diagram 4

Referring to diagram 4 above, add the third petal in the same way. Refer to the project notes for instructions to complete the flower.

LEAVES

Ovate leaves are worked along the following lines:

- The size of the leaf will be determined by the number of beads that you pick up in the first row.
- That number will always be in multiples of two.
- The sides of the leaves are not worked to a point because this would make them diamond shaped, not ovate.
- Depending on the size of the leaf you will work until you have two beads (and one gap) remaining on the side for smaller leaves, or thee beads (and two gaps) forming the final row for larger leaves.
- Within reason, you can make the leaves as large as you like, picking up multiples of two in the first row.
- The smallest viable leaf would involve picking up eight beads in the first row.

Eight-bead leaf

Work this leaf with a single continuous thread that is about 25 cm (10") in length.

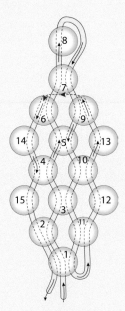

Diagram 1

Pick up a bead of a different colour and GT it again, pulling it down towards the bottom of the thread and leaving a tail of about 12 cm (4¾"). This will act as a stopper bead and will be removed before you attach the leaf to the fabric or bead base.

Referring to diagram 1 above:
1. PU 8 beads
2. GD bead 7
3. PU bead 9, GD bead 5
4. PU bead 10, GD bead 3
5. PU bead 11, GD bead 1
6. GU bead 11
7. PU bead 12, GU bead 10
8. PU bead 13, GU bead 9
9. Following the pink arrows in the diagram, GD bead 6
10. PU bead 14, GD bead 4
11. PU bead 15, GD beads 2 and 1, exiting out of the bottom bead
12. Pulling really tight, tie the two threads together with a double knot

Ten-bead leaf

Work this leaf with a thread that is approximately 30 cm (12") in length.

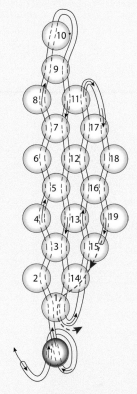

Diagram 1

Pick up a bead of a different colour and GT it again, pulling it to the centre of the length of thread. This will act as a stopper bead and will be removed before you attach the leaf to the fabric or bead base. Work the first half of the leaf with one half of the thread.

Referring to diagram 1 above:
1. PU 10 beads
2. GD bead 9
3. PU bead 11, GD bead 7
4. PU bead 12, GD bead 5
5. PU bead 13, GD bead 3
6. PU bead 14, GD bead 1
7. GU bead 14
8. PU bead 15, GU bead 13
9. PU bead 16, GU bead 12
10. PU bead 17, GU bead 11

11. GD bead 17

12. PU bead 18, GD bead 16

13. PU bead 19, GD bead 15

14. Following the pink arrows in the diagram, GD beads 14 and 1, exiting out of the bottom bead

Remove the needle from the thread that you have been using, pull the stopper bead off the thread and thread the needle with the other half of the thread length.

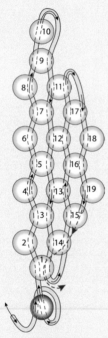

Diagram 2

Referring to diagram 2 above, turn the leaf over and using the second half of the thread:

1. GU bead 2

2. PU bead 20, GU bead 4

3. PU bead 21, GU bead 6

4. PU bead 22, GU bead 8

5. GD bead 22

6. PU bead 23, GD bead 21

7. PU bead 24

8. GD bead 20

9. Following the pink arrow, GD beads 2 and 1 exiting out of the bottom bead

10. Pulling really tight, tie the two threads, depicted by the pink arrows, together with a double knot

Twelve-bead leaf and bigger

Any leaf that has 12 beads and more (working in multiples of two) is worked in the same way as the 10-bead leaf. Referring to the diagrams below:

1. Use a stopper bead and start at bead no. 1 as depicted by the green arrows

2. Beads are numbered according to the sequence by which they are picked up and added to the leaf.

3. Work the first half of the leaf with one half of the thread

4. Work the remaining half of the leaf with the other half of the thread

5. Tie the two tails very tightly together with a double knot

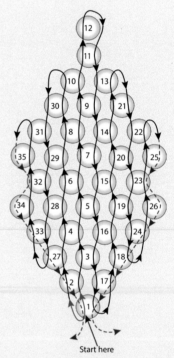

Start here

12-bead leaf

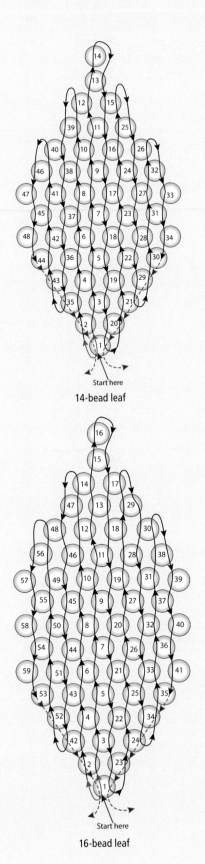

14-bead leaf

16-bead leaf

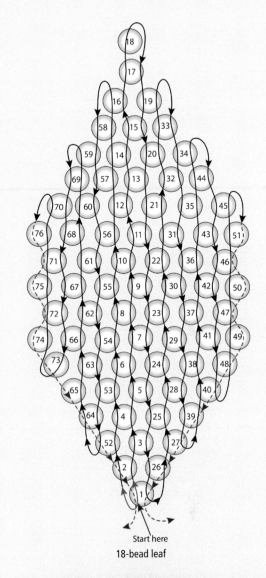

Start here

18-bead leaf

BUDS, CALYXES AND OTHER ELEMENTS

Six-bead bud

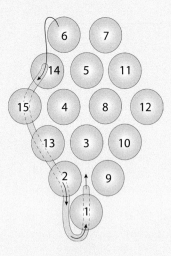

Diagram 1

1. Following the instructions for the first petal of the 6-bead flower, work a petal with one small difference

2. When you have added bead 15, GD bead 13 and 2, then GU bead 1, as indicated in diagram 1 above

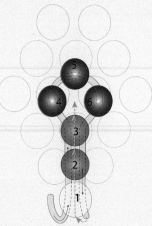

Diagram 2

1. PU beads 2 and 3 for the stalk

2. PU beads 4, 5 and 6 needed for the tip

3. GD beads 2, 3 and bead 1 of the petal

4. Following the green arrow in diagram 2, GU the bead in the petal that sits directly behind bead 3 in the stalk. Encourage the thread to lie at the back of bead one, rather than on the side

5. When you attach the bud to the fabric, work the tail coming out of the bottom of the petal first to place the bud

6. End that thread off and pick up the second tail that comes out of the back of the petal

7. Take that down into the fabric, thereby securing the petal so that it won't swivel

Six- to eight-bead combination flower

This flower has four petals and is combination of 6- and 8-bead petals.

1. Following the instructions for the first petal of the 6-bead flower, work one petal from beads 1 to 15

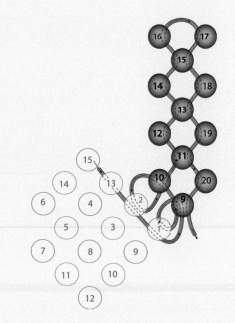

2. PU bead 16

3. GD bead 1, GU bead 16

4. PU bead 17

5. GD bead 2, GU bead 17

6. PU beads 18 to 24

7. GD bead 22, PU bead 25

8. GD bead 20, PU bead 26

9. GD bead 18, PU bead 27

10. GD bead 16

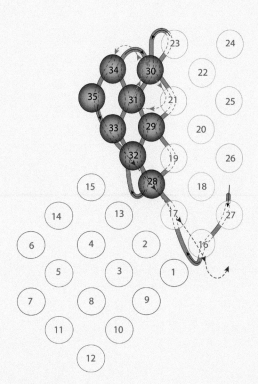

26. GU bead 27

27. PU bead 36, GU bead 26

28. PU bead 37, GU bead 25

29. PU bead 38, GU bead 24

30. GD bead 38

31. PU bead 39, GD bead 37

32. PU bead 40, GD bead 36

33. GU bead 40

34. PU bead 41, GU bead 39

35. PU bead 42

36. Working backwards towards the centre, GD beads 38 and 25

37. GU beads 39 and 38

38. GD bead 42

39. PU bead 43, GD bead 41

40. Following the pink arrow, keep going down the side of the petal through beads 40 to 16, exiting at the bottom of the petal

11. GU bead 17

12. PU bead 28, GU bead 19

13. PU bead 29, GU bead 21

14. PU bead 30, GU bead 23

15. GD bead 30

16. PU bead 31, GD bead 29

17. PU bead 32, GD bead 28

18. GU bead 32

19. PU bead 33, GU bead 31

20. PU bead 34

21. Working backwards towards the centre, GD beads 30 and 21

22. GU beads 31 and 30

23. GD bead 34

24. PU bead 35, GD bead 33

25. Following the pink arrow, keep going down the side of the petal through beads 32 to 16, exiting at the bottom of the petal

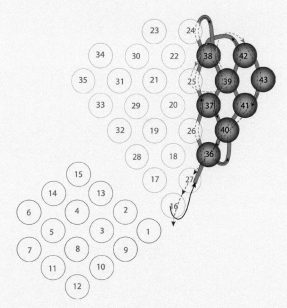

41. Referring to the diagram at the top left of page 56 and steps 1 to 40 on pages 54-55, add a second eight-bead petal, joining it to the previous petal at the two bottom beads as indicated

Eight-bead calyx

This calyx has five leaves and is based on the eight-bead leaf.

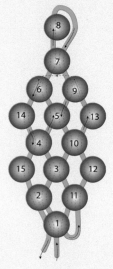

Diagram 1

Following the instructions for an eight-bead leaf, work the first leaf of the calyx.

42. Referring to the diagram below, add a final six-bead petal, joining it to the previous petal at the two bottom beads as indicated

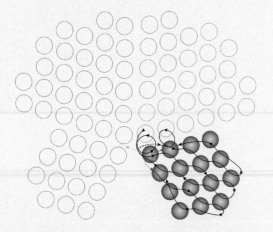

When you attach this element to the fabric, allow the petals to concertina over one another so that once in place, the eight-bead petals come forward and the side six-bead petals lie behind them, vaguely following the shape at the bottom of the tail feather.

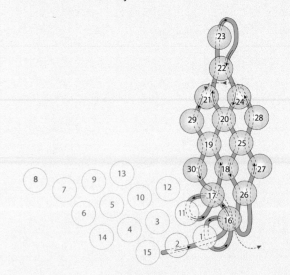

Diagram 2

#Referring to diagram 2 above:
1. PU bead 16
2. GD bead 1, GU bead 16
3. PU bead 17
4. GD bead 11, GU bead 17
5. PU beads 18 to 23, GD bead 22

6. PU bead 24, GD bead 20

7. PU bead 25, GD bead 18

8. PU bead 26, GD bead 16

9. GU bead 26

10. PU bead 27, GU bead 25

11. PU bead 28, GU bead 24

12. Following the pink arrow at the top of the diagram, GD bead 21

13. PU bead 29, GD bead 19

14. PU bead 30, GD bead 17

15. Following the pink arrow at the bottom of the diagram, GD bead 16#

Repeat the above instructions from # to # three times so that you have a total of five leaves in the calyx.

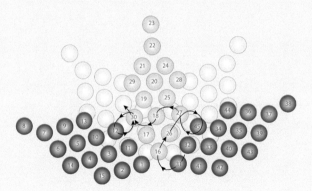

Diagram 3

1. Concertina the five leaves of the calyx so that leaves 2 and 4 sit behind leaves 1, 3 and 5

2. Using the thread that exited the bottom bead of the last leaf worked and referring to diagram 3 above:

3. GU beads 16, 26 and 27 on the side of the middle petal no. 3

4. GD bead 45 of the side petal no. 5

5. GU bead 27 of the middle petal

6. GD bead 18 and GU bead 30 of the middle petal

7. GD bead 12 of side petal no. 1

8. GU bead 30 of the middle petal

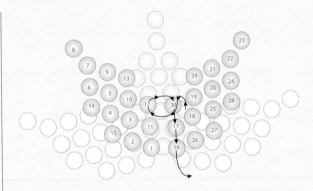

9. Take the needle to the back of the middle petal and turn the calyx over

10. GD bead 30 of petal no. 2

11. GU bead 12 of petal no. 4

12. GD beads 30, 17 and 16 of petal no. 2

Phew. Did you get that? Your calyx is now ready to attach to the fabric. Use the working thread to do that, making sure that you secure the bottom of each calyx leaf. Also secure the calyx further up two or three of the leaves by coming through the fabric, going through a bead that is level with the needle and going back into the fabric.

BEAD EMBROIDERY WORKED DIRECTLY ONTO THE FABRIC

General instructions

- Use a size 10/12 bead embroidery needle or a size 11 sharps quilting needle.
- Unless otherwise instructed, use a single strand of embroidery cotton, doubled over and tied together with a knot.

Attaching a bead with a bead

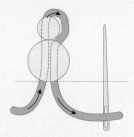

Bring your needle up through the fabric at the correct point. Pick up the larger and then the smaller bead. Return down through the larger bead and tighten the thread. The smaller bead holds the larger bead in place.

Attaching a single bead

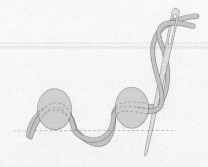

Bring your needle up through the fabric and pick up a bead. Pull the bead down the thread until it touches the fabric. Slide the needle down between the two threads until it touches the bead and go back into the fabric at that point. This will ensure that the length of the stitch holding the bead is correct and is a particularly useful way to attach bugle beads.

Bead couching

Pick up not less than two and not more than five beads. Lay them along the line that you need to follow, estimate about the width of a bead and go through the fabric. Push the beads to the beginning and couch over the thread between the beads, pulling the line into place as you go. Bring the needle up immediately after the last bead and pick up the next group of beads. Keep going in this way. When you reach the end of the line, go through the fabric, catch the thread in the voile backing fabric and return through the same hole. Run the thread through the whole line of beads, going into the fabric at the beginning and tugging the thread to tighten. This pulls the line of beads neatly into place.

Bead circles

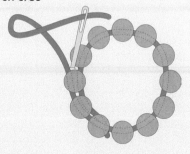

Bring the needle up through the fabric. Pick up as many beads as you require to make the size of circle that you need. From the beginning of the line of beads, take the needle through the first three beads for a second time, making sure that you do not snag the thread with the needle. Go into the fabric, having left enough space to accommodate the three beads that have a double string of thread. Pull through, manipulating the beads so that they form a circle.

With the same thread, work a small couching stitch between the beads, over the circle of thread that holds the bead circle. If you pull that circle of thread out a little as you stitch, the bead circle will form more perfectly.

Bead circle variation

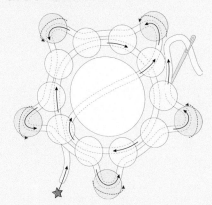

Based on the beadwork daisy chain technique, this variation works best with a 2 mm bead or glass pearl as the central large bead. Referring to the diagram above, pick up 10 beads in the colour of the main circle. Go through the first bead again and pull through so that the beads form a circle. Pick up the larger centre bead. Go up the fifth bead after the bead that you came out of. Pull through. Pick up one second colour bead – this could be the same colour if you like – and go through the next bead in the circle and the bead after that. #Pick up another second colour bead and go through the next two beads in the circle.# Repeat from # to # until you have a total of five second colour beads. Place the circle where it needs to be on the fabric and take the needle into the fabric. Thereafter, come up at each

of the second colour beads, go through the bead to stitch it down and go back into the fabric. End off the thread. Thread the tail at the beginning of the circle onto the needle, take it into the fabric and end off.

Beaded fly stitch

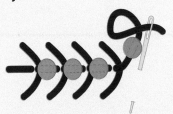

Start at the tip with a 4 mm (¼") straight stitch. Thereafter, come up on the left and go down on the right of the straight stitch, leaving a loop. Come up at the bottom of the straight stitch, catching the loop before you tighten. Pick up a bead and go into the fabric below it, leaving enough room for the bead to sit happily. Leaving a space of about 1 mm on the left side, start the next fly stitch.

Beaded lazy daisy stitch

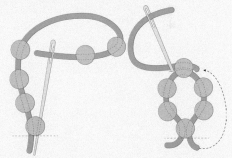

Exit the fabric and pick up four, six or eight beads. Take the needle back through the first of those beads from the top, going back into the fabric at the same time and leaving an odd number of beads to form the loop of beads the make the petal or leaf shape. Bring the needle up through the fabric just to the right of the middle bead at the top. That is the third, fourth or fifth bead. Go through that bead and take the needle back into the fabric just to the left of the bead.

Caged flat-back crystal

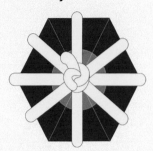

Hold the flat-back crystal in place on the circle drawn for its placement.

1. Use a waste thread that is a completely different colour from the thread you will use to stitch the cage that holds the flat-back crystal in place.
2. Come through the fabric at the top of the crystal. Go into the fabric at the bottom, thus forming a straight stitch that goes down the midline of the crystal.
3. Now work three more stitches to form a star that holds the crystal in place. The first should go over the horizontal midline. The last two go from top right to bottom left and then from top left to bottom right. When working the last two stitches, whip under the intersection of the first two stitches. This holds them all together and stops them from sliding off the crystal.
4. Finish off by coming up one more time and doing a knot over the intersection. This will make it easy to pull these stitches out.

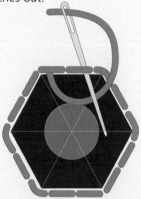

5. Using a single of strand of cotton, do a circle of back stitch around and adjacent to the crystal.

6. Using the same thread, continue by working a detached buttonhole stitch under each backstitch.

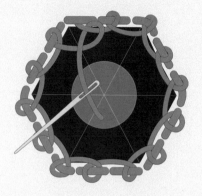

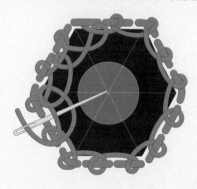

7. When you get back around to the first button-hole stitch, take your needle through the loop of that stitch to secure the end of the row and continue in the opposite direction, working into each of the loops created in the first row.
8. If you are attaching a 20ss crystal it only requires two rows of detached buttonhole stitch.
9. If you are attaching a 34ss crystal, work a third row in the same way.
10. When you reach the end of the final row of detached buttonhole stitch, continue in the same direction, whipping through each of the loops.
11. When you get back to where you started the whipping stitches, pull the thread to tighten the last row and to make sure that it fits snugly against the crystal.

Ease the needle under the detached buttonhole stitches and take it through the fabric to end off.

Linked daisy chain braid

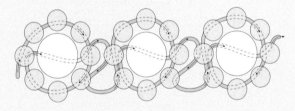

The number of beads in the circle of the daisy chain is always an even number and will vary according to the size of the bead in the centre.

1. PU eight small beads. Pull them down until they are touching the stopper bead at the bottom.
2. GT the first bead again and pull the beads together to make a circle.
3. PU a large bead.
4. Go up the fourth bead away from where you exited the circle.
5. Pull the thread tightly, making sure that the circle sits nicely around the big bead.
6. PU one small bead.
7. Go down the bead below the one that you have just exited.
8. PU one small bead and go up the bead you picked up in (6.) above.
9. You should now have a filled circle with two small beads sitting one above the other to the right of that circle. Those two beads are the start of the next circle.
10. #PU six small beads.
11. Go up the lower bead of the two that are described in (8.) above. Pull the beads together to make a circle.
12. PU a large bead.
13. Go up the fourth bead away from where you exited the circle.
14. Pull the thread tightly, making sure that the circle sits nicely around the big bead.
15. PU one small bead.
16. Go down the bead below the one that you have just exited.
17. PU one small bead and go up the bead you picked up in (6.) above.

18. You should now have a filled circle with two small beads sitting one above the other to the right of that circle. Those two beads are the start of the next circle.#
19. Repeat from # to # until the daisy chain is the required length.
20. Remove the stopper bead that you added to the start and thread that end on a needle.
21. Take the needle through the fabric at the beginning of the line where you wish to place the daisy chain.
22. Thread the other end onto another needle and take the needle through the fabric at the end of the line where you wish to place the daisy chain.
23. Working from both ends alternately, work a couching stitch over the thread between the beads on either side of the circle, as well as a stitch or two over the thread at the point where the circles meet one another.

Simple bead flowers and leaves

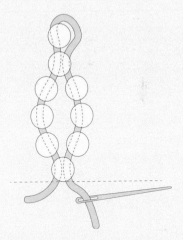

Bring the needle up through the fabric and pick up six* beads. Go down the fifth bead, pick up three* beads and go down the first bead and through the fabric.

*Vary the size of the flower or leaf by adjusting the number of beads picked up.

Needle-lace stitches

GENERAL INSTRUCTIONS

TERMS AND ABBREVIATIONS:
RL: work right to left;
LR: work left to right;
BS: backstitch;
DBH: detached buttonhole stitch;
TB: tulle bar;
Step down: Go into the fabric, burying the thread under the nearest backstitch that is level with the ridge of the detached buttonhole stitch. Come up from under the backstitch at the point where you need to start the next row.

(Find the basic stitches in the embroidery stitch gallery on pages 18 to 31.)

- All the stitches in this gallery are based on needle-lace techniques that have been modified for use as embroidery stitches.
- If you are new to needle-lace techniques, first try the techniques on a scrap of fabric.
- It is almost impossible to create a smooth edge to your needle lace. Try to be as even and smooth as you can but be aware that you will need to either outline the area or modify the edge in some way.
- Always work with your fabric stretched taut in a hoop to prevent puckering.
- Use a size 7 or 8 embroidery needle to work the backstitches (BS) and a size 26 or 28 tapestry needle to work the detached buttonhole stitches (DBH).
- Each shape that you wish to fill with needle lace should be surrounded with backstitch (BS), which can be found in the embroidery stitch gallery. Use these stitches to both anchor the first lace row and to define the area.

- Don't expect your backstitches (BS) to be perfect. It's not a perfect world. Use them as a guide and an anchor only. Adjust your tension and counting to suit the detached buttonhole stitches (DBH), not the backstitch (BS).
- The majority of needle-lace techniques use detached buttonhole stitches (DBH) which can be found in the embroidery stitch gallery.
- Each instruction notes the length of the backstitches (BS) in the top row.
- It usually doesn't matter which direction you choose to stitch your needle lace. You make life easier for yourself if you choose to work the first row on the edge that will give you the longest and straightest row, decreasing or increasing from there.
- LR means working from left to right; RL means working from right to left.
- Always make sure that the beginning and end of each row are approximately level with each other.
- When working further down, always make sure that you space your rows so that the sides of the needle lace are neither bunching up, nor stretching down too far. If you are unsure of where to come up at the beginning of a row, pull the middle section of the row you have just completed down with the point of your needle, see how far it stretches, then come up for the start of your row approximately level with that point.

Working to the shape you need to fill

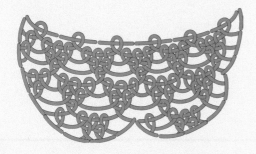

The above diagram is based on needle-lace stitch no. 9 used in the ostrich project in this book.

1. The first row has been worked on the longest line. This means that you won't need to increase, just decrease.

2. At the beginning and end of each row you are cognizant of the pattern you are working, adjusting it to accommodate the space you have available.

3. Note that in some instances, only one or two of the detached buttonhole stitches needed in a group are worked into the loop in the previous row.

4. If you are in doubt as to whether you should work a stitch, it is better to put it there rather than leave it out as you could be in danger of being left with a gaping hole. You never want a hole, if you can avoid it.

Completing the needle-laced area

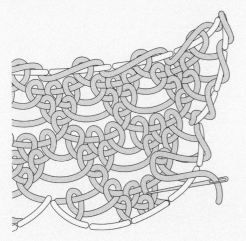

1. Because of the nature and size of the shapes that are filled in this book, go into the fabric at the end of each row, coming up through the fabric at the beginning of the next.

2. When working the last row, come up from under the backstitch in line with where you need to be, work the detached buttonhole stitch and go back into the fabric, burying the needle under the backstitch at the bottom, encouraging the needle lace to stretch evenly down to the bottom.

3. This means that, other than anchoring the stitches in the top row, you will not work through the backstitches on the sides and bottom of the shape.

4. To finish off, whip the backstitch with the same thread used to work the backstitches and the needle lace.

5. Work each portion of the backstitch separately, coming up in the same hole as the backstitch at the beginning and going back into the same hole at the end.

6. If necessary, catch the thread in the voile backing fabric before coming up to start the next whipping line.

NUMBERED STITCHES

Stitch no. 9

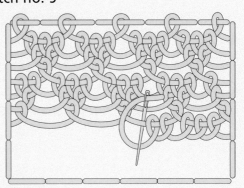

PREPARATION:
BS outline.

TOP ROW STITCH LENGTH:
To accommodate 3 x DBH.

1. Working RL, 1 x DBH in each BS. Step down.

2. #Working LR, 3 x DBH into each loop. Step down.

3. Working RL, [1 x DBH into next loop, 1 x DBH into next loop, miss 1 loop]. Repeat [to] to end. Step down.

4. Working LR, [1 x DBH in small loop, miss large loop]. Repeat [to] to end. Step down. #

Keep working the rows from # to # until you have filled the required space. Follow the instructions for completing the needle-laced area on page 63.

Stitch no. 26 (variation)

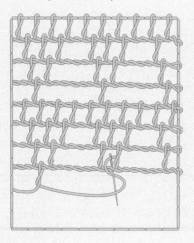

PREPARATION:
BS outline.

TOP ROW STITCH LENGTH:
To accommodate 2 x DBH.

How to work a tulle bar: Take your needle over and under the BS or the loop in the row above, as you would for a DBH. Take the thread under and over the needle to create an additional twist, thereby creating what is referred to in these instructions as a tulle bar (TB).

1. Working LR, 1 x TB (see above) into each BS. Go through the nearest BS down the right-hand side that is level with the ridge of the TB in the row you have just done.

2. Working RL, whip once into each loop. Step down.

3. #Work LR, [1 x TB, 1 x TB, 1 x TB, miss 1 loop]. Repeat [to] to end.

4. Return to the left side as you did in the previous row, described in point 2 above.

5. Working LR, 1 x TB into each small loop.

6. Return to the left side as you did in the previous row, whipping once into each small loop and two or three times into each large loop. Step down.

7. Working LR, 1 x TB into each small loop.

8. Return to the left side as you did in the previous row, whipping three times into each large loop. Step down.

9. Working LR, 4 x TB into each large loop.

10. Working RL, whip once into each loop. Step down. #

Keep working the rows from # to # until you have filled the required space. Follow the instructions for Completing the needle-laced area on page 63.

STITCH VARIATIONS

Needle-lace edging no. 9

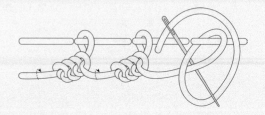

PREPARATION:
BS line along edge.

TOP ROW STITCH LENGTH:
To accommodate 2 x DBH.

1. Miss the first BS and [go under the next one from the top down, catching the loop as you would for a DBH.

2. Go under what will now be a double loop, going

over and catching the working thread to form a DBH at the bottom of the double loop.

3. Do a further 3 x DBH, working up the double loop to a total of 4 x DBH*.]

4. Repeat from [to] until you have worked the buttonhole bar into the last backstitch.

5. Take the thread into the fabric about 0,5 mm to 1 mm away from the end of the backstitch. (This should make the last bar of the lace edging curl around towards the edge of the motif.)

6. It is unlikely that the lace scallops will sit nicely so, to this end, using a single strand of the same colour stranded cotton on a size 10 embroidery needle, couch a small stitch over the thread as indicated by the arrows in the diagram above. Pull the lace down, and use your needle to place the buttonhole bar in a satisfactory position.

*Depending on where you place the edging, you may need to adjust the number of DBH on the double loop. For example, working on a sharp curve or going around a corner may mean that you need to make longer loops which would then require more DBH on those loops. You should adjust as necessary.

Needle-lace filler 1

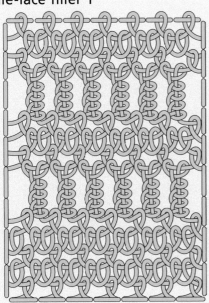

PREPARATION:
BS as directed in project instructions.

TOP ROW STITCH LENGTH:
To accommodate 2 x DBH.

1. Working LR, do 1 x DBH into each BS. Step down.

2. #Working RL, do 2 x DBH into the loops between the DBH in the previous row. Step down.

3. Working LR, do 1 x DBH into the loops that run between each pair of DBH in the previous row.

4. Step down, this time leaving a larger space to accommodate a wider row.

5. Working RL, do 2 x DBH into the loops between the single DBH in the previous row.

6. Turn your work sideways and work 4 x DBH over the thread loop that leads up to the pair of stitches you have just done.

7. Work one of these bars into each of the loops between the single DBH in the previous row.

8. Step down leaving a normal, shorter space.

9. Work single DBH in the loops between the bars in the previous row. Step down.#

10. Keep working the rows from # to # until you have filled the required space.

11. If, towards the end, you find that you will not have enough space to fit in the wider row of buttonhole bars, work only the rows described in points 9, 2 and 3.

Follow the instructions for completing the needle-laced area on page 63.

Filler no. 1 with ribbon inserted

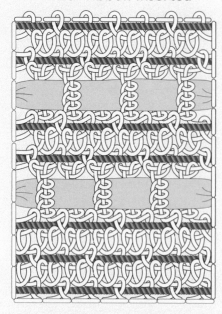

Following the guidelines for filler no. 1 above, fill the shape as directed with needle lace. Referring to the guidelines for inserting silk ribbon and twisted thread at the end of the filler stitch instructions, complete the filler using the recommended materials.

Filler no. 2

PREPARATION:
BS as directed in project instructions.

TOP ROW STITCH LENGTH:
To accommodate 2 x DBH.

1. Working LR, do 1 x DBH into each BS. Step down.
2. #Working RL, do 2 x DBH into the loops between the DBH in the previous row. Step down.
3. Working LR, do 1 x DBH into the loops that run between each pair of DBH in the previous row.
4. Step down, this time leaving a larger space to accommodate a wider ribbon insertion row.
5. Working RL, do 2 x DBH into the loops between the single DBH in the previous row.
6. Turn your work sideways and work 2 x DBH over the thread loop that leads up to the pair of stitches you have just done.
7. Work one of these bars into each of the loops between the single DBH in the previous row.
8. Step down leaving a normal, shorter space.
9. Work single DBH in the loops between the bars in the previous row. Step down.#
10. Keep working the rows from # to # until you have filled the required space.
11. If, towards the end, you find that you will not have enough space to fit in the wider row of button-hole bars, work only the rows described in points 9, 2 and 3.

Follow the instructions for completing the needle-laced area on page 63. Referring to the guidelines for inserting silk ribbon and twisted thread at the end of the filler stitch instructions, complete the filler using the recommended materials.

Filler no. 3

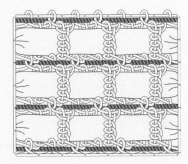

PREPARATION:
BS as directed in project instructions.

TOP ROW STITCH LENGTH:
To accommodate 2 x DBH.

1. Working LR, do 1 x DBH into each BS. Step down leaving a space large enough to accommodate a ribbon insertion row (i.e. 2 mm plus a bit of wiggle room for above and below the ribbon).
2. #Working RL, do 2 x DBH into the loops between the single DBH in the previous row.
3. Turn your work sideways and work 4 x DBH over the thread loop that leads up to the pair of stitches you have just done.
4. Work one of these bars into each of the loops between the single DBH in the previous row.
5. Step down, leaving a normal, shorter space.
6. Work single DBH in the loops between the bars in the previous row. Step down, leaving a larger space for ribbon insertion.#
7. Keep working the rows from # to # until you have filled the required space.
8. If, towards the end, you find that you will not have enough space to fit in the wider row of buttonhole bars, work a few rows of single detached buttonhole stitches as described in 6 above.

Follow the instructions for completing the needle-laced area on page 63. Referring to the guidelines for inserting silk ribbon and twisted thread at the end of the filler stitch instructions, complete the filler using the recommended materials.

INSERTING SILK RIBBON AND TWISTED THREAD INTO YOUR NEEDLE-LACE FILLER:
Following the guidelines for working with twisted thread on page 31, and working with a single strand of thread, twist a 2 m (2½ yd) length of thread to create a cord. The cord will, effectively, comprise four twisted threads.

1. Threading it onto a chenille needle, working with the rows that consist of single detached buttonhole stitches, as depicted in the stitch diagram, bring it up at the side, trying to come up from under the bac stitch.
2. Weave over and under the single detached buttonhole stitches, taking it back in under the backstitch on the other side.

TIP

A sharp (chenille) needle has been suggested to make it easier to bring the twisted cord through the fabric. You could rethread it into a large tapestry needle to do the weaving. It is, however, usually enough to just be careful not to snag the threads with the sharp point of the needle.

3. Weave the silk ribbon through the rows that comprise the bars, as depicted in the diagram above left, in the same way. It is important to make the ribbon lie as flat as possible.

Needle-weaving techniques

Basic: double weaving

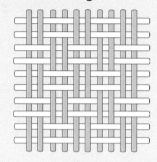

Warp: Colour 1
Weft: Colour 1 – or a different colour (pattern repeat 4 rows)

1. O2, U2
2. O2, U2
3. U2, O2
4. U2, O2

Basic: single weaving

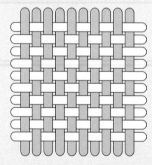

Warp: Colour 1
Weft: Colour 1 – or a different colour (pattern repeat 2 rows)

1. O1, U1
2. U1, O1

Single weaving: shading variation

Working with a single strand of stranded cotton, create the warp stitches from top to bottom making them between 1 and 2 mm apart. Following the instructions above for each row of single weaving, work the weft stitches about the same distance apart. You will usually be working freehand to fill an area and this means that the length of your warp and weft stitches could vary according to the shape you choose to fill. This may mean that some of your warp stitches would be broken. Referring to the image above, if you would like to create an impression of changing shades, work a few of the warp and weft stitches in a close but darker (or lighter) colour.

Checks and stripes no. 1

Warp: 4 x colour 1; 4 x colour 2
Weft: 4 x colour 2; 3 x colour 1 (pattern repeat 7 rows)

COLOUR 2
1. (O2, U1) O3, U1
2. (O1, U1) O3, U1
3. (U1) O3, U1
4. O3, U1

COLOUR 1
5. (U3) O1, U3
6. (U2) O1, U3
7. (U1) O1, U3

Weaving checks and stripes no. 4

Warp: 4 x colour 1; 4 x colour 2
Weft: 2 x colour 1; 2 x colour 2 (pattern repeat 4 rows)

COLOUR 1
1. (U2) O1, U2
2. O1, U2

COLOUR 2
3. (U2) O1, U2
4. (U1) O1, U2

Checks and stripes no. 6

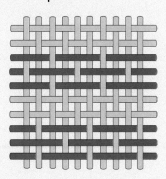

Warp: Colour 1
Weft: Colour 1; Colour 2 (pattern repeat 10 rows)

COLOUR 1
1. O1, U1
2. U1, 01

COLOUR 2
3. O3, U1
4. (O1, U1) O3, U1
5. O3, U1

COLOUR 1
6. U1, 01
7. O1, U1

COLOUR 2
8. (U1) O3, U1
9. (O2, U1) O3, U1
10. (U1) O3, U1

Checks and stripes no. 9

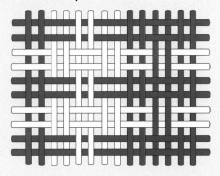

Warp: 6 x colour 1; 6 x colour 2
Weft: 2 x colour 1; 2 x colour 2 (pattern repeat 4 rows)

COLOUR 1
1. (U2) O2, U2
2. (U2) O2, U2

COLOUR 2
3. O2, U2
4. O2, U2

Checks and stripes no. 13

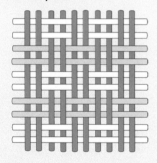

Warp: Colour 1
Weft: Colour 2; Colour 3 (pattern repeat 4 rows)

COLOUR 2
1. (U2) O2, U2
2. (U2) O2, U2

COLOUR 3
3. O2, U2
4. O2, U2

Checks and stripes: tartan variation

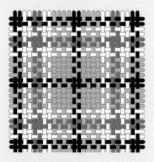

To create a pattern that resembles tartan, the colour sequence is identical for both the warp and the weft. Following the guidelines for single weaving at the beginning of this techniques gallery, the colour sequence is as under and the pattern repeat is 24 rows.

1. Rows 1 and 2: Colour 1
2. Rows 3 and 4: Colour 2
3. Rows 5 and 6: Colour 3
4. Rows 7 and 8: Colour 2
5. Rows 9 to 12: Colour 4
6. Rows 13 and 14: Colour 1
7. Rows 15 to 18: Colour 2
8. Rows 19 and 20: Colour 2
9. Rows 21 and 22: Colour 3
10. Rows 23 and 24: Colour 2

Pattern no. 2

Warp: Colour 1
Weft: Colour 2 (pattern repeat 14 rows)

1. (O1, U3) O1, U1, O1, U3, O2, U3
2. (O2, U3) O1, U3, O4, U3
3. (U1) O2, U2, O1, U2, O2, U2
4. (U2) O2, U3, O2, U4
5. (O1, U2) O2, U1, O2, U2, O2, U2
6. (O2, U2) O3, U2, O4, U2
7. (U1) O1, U3, O1, U3, O1, U2
8. (U1) O1, U1, O1, U1, O1, U1, O1, U1, O1, U2
9. Repeat row 7
10. Repeat row 6
11. Repeat row 5
12. Repeat row 4
13. Repeat row 3
14. Repeat row 2

Texture no. 2

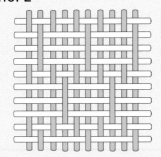

Warp: Colour 1
Weft: Colour 2 (pattern repeat 8 rows)

1. O1, U1
2. *(U1) O3, U1*
3. Repeat * to *
4. Repeat * to *
5. O1, U1
6. #(O2, U1) O3, U1#
7. Repeat # to #
8. Repeat # to #

Texture no. 3

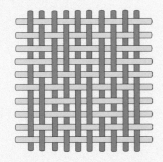

Warp: Colour 1
Weft: Colour 1; Colour 2   (pattern repeat 8 rows)

COLOUR 1
1. O1, U1
2. (U1) O1, U1

COLOUR 2
3. O2, U2
4. O2, U2

COLOUR 1
5. O1, U1
6. (U1) O1, U1

COLOUR 2
7. (U2) O2, U2
8. (U2) O2, U2

Texture no. 5

Warp: Colour 1
Weft: Colour 2 (pattern repeat 4 rows)

1. (O1, U2) O2, U2
2. (U2) O2, U2
3. (U1) O2, U2
4. O2, U2

Texture no. 6

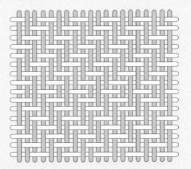

Warp: Colour 1
Weft: Colour 2 (pattern repeat 16 rows)

1. (O1, U2) O2, U2
2. O2, U2
3. (U1) O2, U2
4. (U2) O2, U2
5. (O1, U2) O2, U2
6. O2, U2
7. (U1) O2, U2
8. (U2) O2, U2
9. (O1, U2) O2, U2
10. (U2) O2, U2
11. (U1) O2, U2
12. O2, U2
13. (O1, U2) O2, U2
14. (U2) O2, U2
15. (U1) O2, U2
16. O2, U2

Texture no. 8

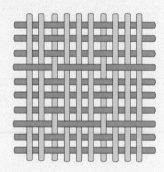

Warp: Colour 1
Weft: Colour 1 (pattern repeat 4 rows)

1. (U3) O1, U3
2. (U3) O1, U3
3. (U3) O1, U3
4. O3, U1

Texture no. 9

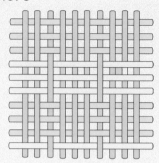

Warp: Colour 1
Weft: Colour 1 or 2 (pattern repeat 6 rows)

1. (U3) O1, U3
2. (U3) O1, U3
3. (U3) O1, U3
4. O3, U1
5. O3, U1
6. O3, U1

Texture no. 10

Warp: Colour 1
Weft: Colour 1 or 2 (pattern repeat 4 rows)

1. O3, U3
2. O3, U3
3. O3, U3
4. U3, O3

Norman

TORTOISE

Dimensions: 207 x 200 mm (8$\frac{1}{8}$ x 7$\frac{7}{8}$")

From Ancient Greece to the Far East, Africa and everywhere else
for that matter, tortoises are the stuff of legends and popular culture.
Slow, dependable and patient, with a long lifespan,
they are symbols of longevity and stability.

Materials

FABRIC

450 x 450 mm (18 x 18") natural coloured cotton linen blend base fabric

450 x 450 mm (18 x 18") off-white cotton voile backing fabric

EMBROIDERY FRAME

14" Morgan plastic hoop

NEEDLES

Size 7 Embroidery needles
Size 10 Embroidery needles
Size 11 Sharps quilting needles
Size 24 Tapestry needles
Size 26 Tapestry needles

THREADS AND BEADS

DMC STRANDED COTTON

150	Ultra Very Dark Dusty Rose
151	Very Light Dusty Rose
153	Very Light Violet
550	Very Dark Violet
553	Medium Violet
554	Light Violet
610	Dark Drab Brown
611	Drab Brown
612	Light Drab Brown
924	Very Dark Grey Blue
926	Medium Grey Blue
928	Very Light Grey Blue
934	Black Avocado Green
3033	Very Light Mocha Brown
3051	Dark Green Grey
3052	Medium Green Grey
3053	Green Grey
3326	Light Rose
3346	Hunter Green
3347	Medium Yellow Green
3348	Light Yellow Green
3350	Ultra Dark Dusty Rose
3354	Light Dusty Rose
3731	Very Dark Dusty Rose
3733	Dusty Rose
3781	Dark Mocha Brown
3782	Light Mocha Brown
3823	Ultra Pale Yellow
3854	Medium Autumn Gold
3855	Light Autumn Gold
3856	Ultra Very Light Mahogany

DMC PERLE #12

437	Light Tan
640	Very Dark Beige Grey
3033	Very Light Mocha Brown

DMC DENTELLES #80

ECRU	Ecru
210	Medium Lavender
553	Medium Violet
3347	Medium Yellow Green
3348	Light Yellow Green

SUPERLON BEADING THREAD AA

Cream
Olive

MIYUKI BEADS

2g	15° 454	Metallic Dark Plum Iris
2g	15° 455	Metallic Dark Variegated Iris
4g	15° 459	Metallic Olive
2g	15° 641	Rose Bronze Silver Lined Alabaster
2g	15° 645	Dark Rose Silver Lined Alabaster
4g	15° 650	Rustic Grey Silver Lined Alabaster
4g	15° 1631	Semi Frosted Silver Lined Saffron
6g	15° 2442	Crystal Ivory Gold Luster
2g	DPF 23	Hot Pink Lined Crystal
2g	DPF 34	Red Lined Dark Topaz
2g	DPF 40	Sparkle Purple Lined Crystal
2g	DP452	Metallic Dark Blue Iris

PRECIOSA VIVA 12 FLAT-BACK CRYSTALS

10 pieces 34ss Light Rose AB

GENERAL INSTRUCTIONS

- Stretch the fabric print over a 14" hoop. I worked the original on a 14/12" Morgan lap stand.
- Make sure that the print is taut. This will improve the quality of your work.
- Assume that threads are stranded cotton unless otherwise described.
- If you are unsure of any of the stitches, practise on a scrap of fabric before working on the project.
- When working with stranded cotton, use two strands in a size 7 embroidery needle, unless otherwise advised.
- If advised to use single strand, work with a size 10 embroidery needle.
- Work with a single strand, doubled over and threaded onto a size 11 sharps quilting needle for all bead embroidery stitches.
- Work with single strands of Perle and Dentelles threads.
- Use a size 7 embroidery needle when you work the warp stitches in the weaving.
- Use a size 24 or 26 tapestry needle for the weaving weft stitches and a size 26 tapestry needle for the needle-lace detached buttonhole stitches.

STITCHING INSTRUCTIONS

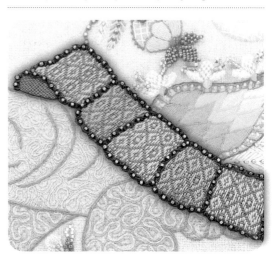

The bridge that lies at the bottom of the floral carapace is filled with woven blocks. Stitching these blocks can become tedious and a good plan is to work them from time to time, rewarding yourself with something interesting in between.

1. Each block is filled with needle weaving pattern no. 2 (*see* page 70).
2. Alternate the colours of the blocks.
3. Working from the left, work the first block.
4. Use perle #12 3033 for the warp stitches and perle #12 640 for the weft stitches.
5. Moving to the next block, use perle #12 3033 for the warp stitches and perle #12 437 for the weft stitches.
6. Fill the small space between the shell and the head of the tortoise with single weaving using perle #12 640.
7. When you have completed the blocks and surrounding embroidery, work a line of knotted cable chain stitch around each block using two strands of 3781.
8. Using the same thread, stitch a single bead 15° 650 in each loop of the chain.

21. The small tail on the other end of the tortois is worked in the same way, using the same colours.

The front and back legs are worked in the same way with one small difference.

9. Pad the eye with small stem stitch using two strands of 3033. Work in a circle from the outside to the centre, leaving a small empty area in the middle.

10. Using a single strand of the same thread, work satin stitch over the padding from the outside to the same point in the centre.

11. Using 610, stitch a single bead 15° 650 into the centre of the eye.

12. Using two strands of 610 ,work a backstitch outline around the eye.

13. With the same thread, work backstitch on the eyebrow, eye folds and wrinkles in the neck.

14. Following the guidelines for Vermicelli couching and the two-thread variation in the embroidery stitch gallery, fill the head and neck, taking the needle under the brown backstitches where you need to.

15. Use two strands of 612 couched down with a single strand of the same thread for the first sequence.

16. The second sequence is worked in single strands of the same thread.

17. When you have completed both sequences, whip the brown backstitch lines, including around the eye, using two strands of 610.

18. Using a single strand of 3781, work outline stitch along the outside of the curve adjacent to each line of whipped backstitch.

19. Using 610, outline the head and neck with whipped backstitch.

20. Using a single strand of 3781, work outline stitch along the outside edge adjacent to the whipped backstitch.

22. Use two strands of 612 couched down with a single strand of the same thread for the first sequence.

23. The second sequence is worked in single strands of the thread 611.

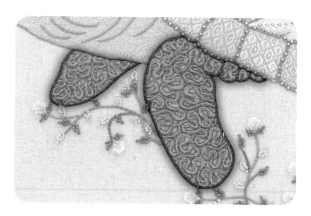

24. Using 610, outline each leg and the leg folds with whipped backstitch.

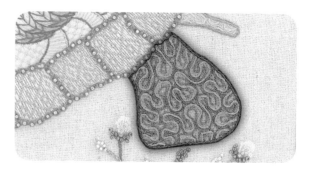

25. Using a single strand of 3781, work outline stitch along the outside edge adjacent to the whipped backstitch.

Moving to the decorated carapace, start with the bunch of berries at top right.

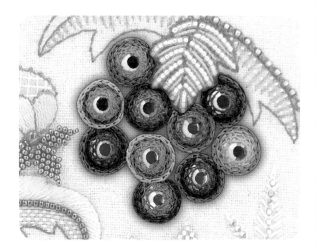

In the diagram below, each berry has been given a number. To determine which thread to use for each berry, refer to the table below.

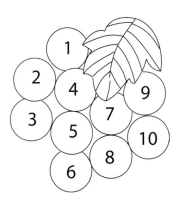

Berry no.	To attach crystal (single strand)	Chain stitch first row	Chain stitch second row
1	3731	3350	3731
2	3731	3350	3326
3	150	150	3350
4	3350	3350	150
5	3731	3731	3733
6	3350	3350	150
7	3350	3350	3731
8	150	150	3731
9	150	150	3731
10	3326	3326	3733

26. Referring to the guidelines for attaching caged flat-back crystals in the bead embroidery techniques gallery, place a 34ss Light Rose AB flat-back crystal in the centre of each circle using a single strand of cotton.

27. Work two concentric circles of chain stitch around each caged crystal using a double strand of the thread noted in the table below left.

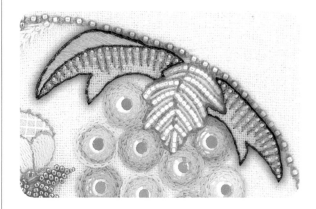

28. Starting at the tip and using a single strand of 3051, work downward facing up and down buttonhole stitch on the vein of each of these leaves. Vary the length of the stitch according to the space available in the bottom half of the leaf.

29. Using a single strand of 3348, work two rows of single wrap French knots in the spaces between the spokes of the up and down buttonhole stitch.

30. In the middle section of the leaf, where the spokes are longer, work a third, shorter row of knots.

31. Fill the top half of the left side leaf with diagonal satin stitch that faces into the vein. Use a single strand of 3053.

32. Using a single strand of 934, work outline stitch up the vein of each leaf.

33. Outline the leaf in the same way, using the same thread.

34. Using thread 3348, bead couch a line of beads 15° 1631 on each of the veins within the leaf at the top of the berries.

35. Using two strands of 3347, place a bullion knot in the spaces between the bead lines.

36. Using single strand of 934, define the leaf by working outline stitch around the entire leaf.

Moving to the lower half of the carapace, work on the flower on the right.

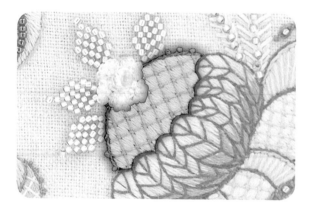

37. Pad the top half of this bloom with stem stitch using two strands of 3033.

38. With a single strand of the same thread, work vertical satin stitch over the padding.

39. Referring to the image above, work trellis couching over the satin stitch using a single strand of 3053.

40. Using two strands of 3052, work outline stitch along the outer edge this area.

41. Using the same thread, work a single wrap French knot at intervals adjacent to the outline stitch.

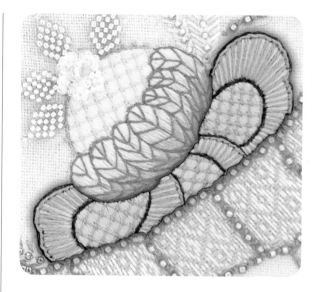

42. Moving to the leaves at the bottom of the bloom, pad the space in the centre of each leaf with stem stitch using 3033.

43. With a single strand of the same thread, work vertical satin stitch over the padding.

44. Referring to the image above, work trellis couching over the satin stitch using a single strand of 3052.

45. Using two strands of 3347, work striped blanket stitch in the spaces that form the edge of each leaf. Using the colour image as your guide, fan the stitches around each edge, leaving a small space between the spokes of each stitch.

46. Using two strands of 3348, starting at the base, work a straight stitch between the blanket stitches, burying the end of the straight stitch under the ridge of the blanket stitch.

47. With a single strand of 934, work outline stitch in the ditch between the centre space and the blanket stitch edge of each leaf.

48. Using the same thread, work a fine line of outline stitch adjacent to the outside of the ridge of the blanket stitch that forms the outside edge of each leaf.

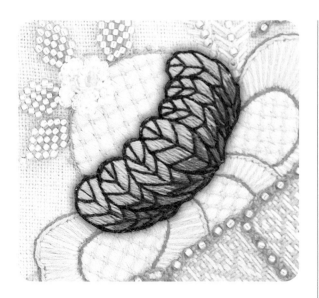

49. Save for the outline, work each identical shape until completion so that you don't lose the outline of each shape as you proceed.

50. Using two strands of 3782 (the same colour as the background fabric), pad the shape with horizontal satin stitch.

51. Work vertical long and short stitch over the padding, starting at the base with a single strand of 553 shading through 554 to 153 at the tip.

52. Using a single strand of 550, work fly stitch over the shading, from tip to base.

53. When you have completed the shapes and using the same thread, work outline stitch all the way around the centre shape.

54. Thereafter, outline the exposed edge of the other shapes in the same way.

Because your thread would be inclined to snag while stitching, you might like to consider making the three-dimensional beaded elements that are at the top of this flower, but only attaching them to the fabric later.

55. Referring to three-dimensional beaded elements on page 32, it is advisable to read the general instructions before you start making three-dimensional leaves and flowers.

56. Work a four-bead flower using beads 15° 2442 and cream beading thread.

57. Work four 10-bead ovate leaves using beads 15° 1631 and olive beading thread.

58. Following the general instructions for attaching beaded elements to the fabric on page 34 and using the colour image above as your guide, attach the leaves first.

59. Thereafter, attach the flower to the small circle at the top of the main part of the bloom.

60. When it is attached, come up in the centre of the flower with the beading thread that is still threaded on the beading needle, pick up drop bead DPF 40, go back into the fabric and end off the thread.

61. Using two strands of 3855, work wheatear stitch down each of the areas that comprise the fern leaves radiating from the flower you have just completed.

62. Using two strands of 3854, place a straight stitch between the outside spokes of the wheatear stitch.

63. Using 3781, stitch a single bead 15° 641 into each loop created by the wheatear stitch.

Three blue-grey and pink berries feature in the tortoise shell. They are worked in the same way.

64. Fill each petal with raised stem stitch.

65. Use two strands of 3354 for the middle petal and 3733 for those on either side of it.

66. When you have completed the surrounding embroidery, define each petal with outline stitch using a single strand of 150.

67. Continuing with the same thread, place a line of single-wrap French knots on the outline of the small dot at the junction created by the base of the petals.

68. Come up in the middle of the circle of French knots, pick up drop bead DPF 34, go back into the fabric and end off the thread.

69. Pad the bottom half of the berry with stem stitch using two strands of 926.

70. Using a single strand of the same thread, work vertical satin stitch over the padding.

71. Referring to the image above, work trellis couching over the satin stitch using a single strand of 928.

72. Using two strands of 924, work outline stitch adjacent to the outer edge of the lower part of the berry.

73. Using the same thread, work a single wrap French knot at intervals adjacent to the outline stitch.

74. With thread 924, bead couch a line of beads 15° 455 to create the stem of the berry.

75. Stop when you reach the small circle at the base of the berry and, using the same thread, stitch a drop bead DP 452 into the middle of that circle.

76. Each berry has beaded leaves radiating from the circle at the tip. The berry at the bottom of the carapace needs 8-bead ovate leaves whilst the two at the top require 10-bead ovate leaves.

77. Work the leaves with beads 15° 459 and olive beading thread.

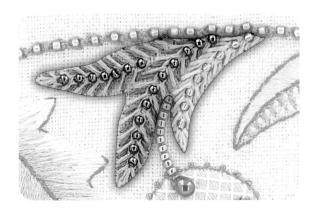

78. At the base of each of the berry stems are beaded wheatear stitch leaves.

79. Using 3051 for the green leaves and 3855 for the yellow, work wheatear stitch over each of the areas that comprise the fern leaves.

80. Using two strands of 3053 for the green and 3854 for the yellow leaves, place a straight stitch between the outside spokes of the wheatear stitch.

81. Stitch a single bead into each loop created by the wheatear stitch.

82. Use thread 3051 and bead 15° 459 for the green leaves.

83. Use thread 3781 and bead 15° 641 for the yellow leaves.

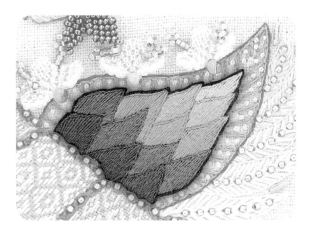

84. Each of these shapes is filled in the same way. Start at the tip, working in rows, finishing at the base.

85. Fill the shape with horizontal satin stitch padding using two strands of thread.

86. Over the padding, work fine, close buttonhole stitch with the ridge on the upper side.

87. In the second and subsequent rows make sure that the ridge of the buttonhole stitch hides the raw edge in the row above.

88. Use 151 for the single shape in the top row, followed by 3354, 3326, 3731 and 3350 as you work each row to the base of the flower.

89. When you have completed the surrounding embroidery and other than the bottom edge, work fine outline stitch around the outside edge of the buttonhole petals. Use a single strand of 150.

90. On the outer right-hand side of this flower are beaded wheatear stitch leaves worked in the same way as before. When you have completed all of them, outline each one with outline stitch using a single strand of thread.

91. Starting at the top, the first two leaves use 3854 for the wheatear stitch and 3856 for the straight stitches. Outline with 3854.

92. Work the wheatear stitch of the third leaf with 3855, using 3854 for the straight stitch and outlining with a single strand of 3854.

93. Work the wheatear stitch of the two leaves at the bottom with 3823, using 3855 for the straight stitch and outlining with a single strand of 3855.

94. Stitch a single bead into each loop created by the wheatear stitch using thread 3781 and bead 15° 641.

95. Using the colour image as your guide, work a bullion lazy daisy stitch in the gaps between the wheatear stitches using two strands of 3347.

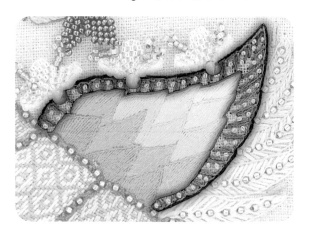

96. Starting at the base on the right-hand side, create the border around the central pink area with inward facing up and down buttonhole stitch using two strands of 3051.

97. Using a single strand of 3348, work single wrap French knots in the spaces between the spokes of the up and down buttonhole stitch.

98. Start with a single knot, increasing to two knots where the space is wider.

99. Define the outer edge of the border with outline stitch worked with a single strand of 934.

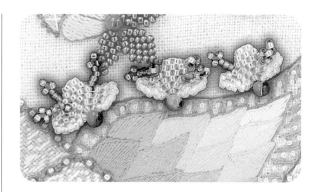

100. Referring to the instructions for the six-bead flower on page 37, work three flowers with only three petals each using beads 15° 2442 and cream beading thread.

101. Attach the flower to the fabric so that the bottom beads of each petal sit on the line of the small circles provided, leaving enough space for the drop bead in the centre.

102. If your beading tension has been tight, the two side petals should curl up on the bottom edges. If would do no harm, however, when attaching the flower, to take the needle and thread through the far right (or left) bead of the petal. Bring it up through the fabric, going in between the beads, go through the bead and go back into the fabric, finding your way down through the beads. Pull tight to make sure that the petal does curl, encouraging it with your fingers to do so.

103. Using the same thread, come up in the centre, pick up a drop bead DPF 23 and go down again through the fabric.

104. Still using the beading thread, create stamens coming out from behind the petals.

105. Pick up three to five beads 15° 650 and three beads 15° 641. Return down the three to five beads that comprise the stalk, going back into the fabric and coming up where you want the next one to be placed.

106. Moving to the leaf that sits in the centre of the carapace, fill the top side highlighted in the image with long and short stitch shading.

107. Starting close to the vein, use single strand of 3782, shading through 3033 to 3348 on the edge.

108. Define the outer edge with outline stitch using a single strand of 3346.

109. Referring to the instructions for double weaving on page 68, use Dentelles #80 553 for the warp stitches which are placed over the shortest side.

110. The weft stitches are worked with a double row of Dentelles #80 Ecru, alternating with a double row of Dentelles #80 210.

111. Define the outer edge with outline stitch using a single strand of 550.

112. With the same thread, bead couch a line of beads 15° 454 up the vein, continuing the line along the loop of the tendril.

113. Fill the centre of this fruit with woven trellis couching.

114. Following the guidelines in the embroidery stitch gallery, use two strands of 3033 for shade 1, the first two layers.

115. Use two strands of 3731 for the couching stitch, referred to as shade 2.

116. Use two strands of 3033 for the weaving, referred to as thread shades 3 and 4.

117. When you have completed the surrounding embroidery, work outline stitch in the ditch between the woven trellis and the plump, bottom part of the fruit using a single strand of 3350.

118. Following the shape of the area, pad this plump part of the fruit with semi-circles of stem stitch. Using two strands of 3782, start on the inside working out to the outer edge.

119. Work long and short stitch shading over the padding, starting at the bottom of the fruit with a single strand of 3854, shading through 3855 to 3823 in the middle of the area.

120. Continue shading up to the top edge with 3855 to 3854 adjacent to the woven trellis in the centre of the fruit.

121. With a single strand of 3823, work basic trellis couching over the long and short stitch shading using the colour image on page 85 as your guide.

128. Fill the green leaf with needle weaving texture no. 9.

129. Working them over the long side, use dentelles #80 3347 for the warp stitches.

130. The weft stitches are worked horizontally over the short side using dentelles #80 3348.

131. Fill the lower purple petal with basic double weaving using Dentelles #80 553 for the warp stitches which are placed over the shortest side.

132. The weft stitches are worked with a double row of Dentelles #80 Ecru alternating with a double row of Dentelles #80 210.

133. Using two strands of 3782 (the same colour as the background fabric), pad the top purple leaf.

134. Work vertical long and short stitch over the padding, starting at the base with a single strand of 553 shading through 554 to 153 at the tip.

135. Using a single strand of 550, work fly stitch over the shading, from tip to base.

136. When you have completed the shapes and using the same thread, define the outer edge of each purple leaf with outline stitch using a single strand of 550.

137. Define the green leaf with outline stitch using a single strand of 934.

122. Moving to the leaf on the right-hand side of the fruit, pad the inside half with rows of stem stitch using two strands of 3346.

123. With a single strand of the same thread, work diagonal satin stitch over the padding, starting at the tip and working to the base of the leaf.

124. Fill the outside half of the leaf with long and short stitch shading. This is not padded.

125. Starting adjacent to the vein and working from tip to base, use a single strand of 3346, shading through 3347 to 3348 on the outer edge.

126. With a single strand of 934, work outline stitch up the vein.

127. With the same thread, work intermittent outline stitch around the outer edge of both halves of the leaf, using the image above to guide you.

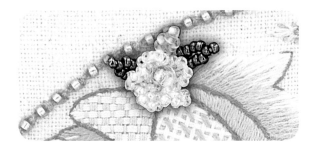

138. Work a four-bead flower using beads 15° 2442 and cream beading thread.

139. Follow the general instructions for attaching beaded elements to the fabric on page 34.

140. When it is attached, come up in the centre of the flower with the beading thread that is still threaded on the beading needle, pick up a drop bead DPF 40, go back into the fabric and end off the thread.

141. Following the guidelines for simple flowers and leaves on page 61, placing them with reference to the above colour image, work a seven-bead and a six-bead leaf with 15° 459. The lighter green leaf is worked with 15° 1631 and is a six-bead leaf. Use olive beading thread.

142. Starting adjacent to the last block of the bridge on the right of the design and ending adjacent to the first block on the left, finish the carapace by working a line of knotted cable chain stitch on the outside line of the shell, using two strands of 3781.

143. Using the same thread, stitch a single bead 15° 650 in each loop of the chain.

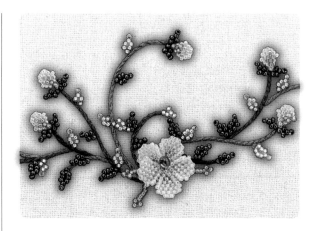

144. Referring to the main colour image of the design, work all the stems in Portuguese knotted stem stitch using two strands of thread.

145. Work the brown stems with 3781, the medium green stems with 3051 and the dark green stems with 934.

146. Referring to the three-dimensional beaded elements on page 32, make an eight-bead flower using beads 15° 2442 and cream beading thread. Do not work the stamens in the middle of the flower.

147. Stitch the flower over the meeting point of the stems in the centre.

148. When it is attached, come up in the centre of the flower with the beading thread that is still threaded on the beading needle, pick up a drop bead DPF 40, and go back into the fabric.

149. Use the remaining thread to work three twigs that come out from under the petals of the flower. They should be of varying lengths using beads 15° 650 for the stalks and three beads 15° 645 for the tips.

150. Still referring to the main colour image of the design, work six-bead buds following the guidelines in the bead embroidery gallery. Use beads 15° 2442 for the petals, 15° 650 for the stamen stalk and three beads 15° 645 for the tip.

151. Work five- to seven-bead simple leaves radiating from all the branches and in some instances, on the tips. Using olive beading thread work some with beads 15° 459 and others with 15° 1631.

Audrey

OSTRICH

Dimensions: 310 x 190 mm (12³/₁₆ x 7½")

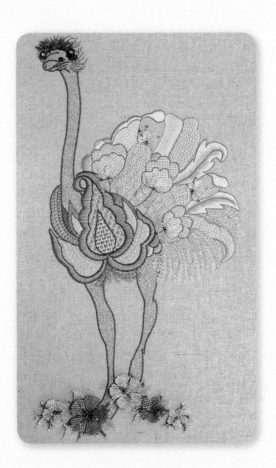

The largest of the flightless birds and native to Africa, the ostrich was originally
farmed for its decorative feathers. Using artistic licence, I worked this project
in the delicate shades of the Little Karoo – a semi-desert region of
Southern Africa that is home to most of the ostrich farms in that area.

Materials

FABRIC

450 x 450 mm (18 x 18") natural coloured cotton linen blend base fabric
450 x 450 mm (18 x 18") off-white cotton voile backing fabric

EMBROIDERY FRAME

16" x 12" stretcher bars

NEEDLES

Size 7 Embroidery needles
Size 10 Embroidery needles
Size 11 Sharps quilting needles
Size 24 Tapestry needles
Size 26 Tapestry needles
Size 12 Long beading needle

THREADS AND BEADS

DMC STRANDED COTTON

644	Medium Beige Grey
3032	Medium Mocha Brown
3033	Very Light Mocha Brown (x 2)
3781	Dark Mocha Brown
3782	Light Mocha Brown (x 3)
3790	Ultra Dark Beige Grey (x 2)

DMC DENTELLES #80

| ECRU | Ecru |
| 3033 | Very Light Mocha Brown |

SUPERLON BEADING THREAD AA

Cream
Ash

MIYUKI BEADS

Size 15°

4g	650	Rustic Grey SL Alabaster
4g	1527	Sparkle Celery Lined Crystal
4g	2442	Crystal Ivory Gold Luster

Size 11°

| 2g | 577 | Butter Cream SL Alabaster |

Size 11° Delica Beads

4g	1451	SL Pale Cream Opal
2g	1459	SL Shell Opal
2g	1731	Beige Lined Opal

PRECIOSA VIVA 12 FLAT-BACK CRYSTALS

2 pieces   20ss Smoke Topaz AB

CZECH FIRE POLISHED BEADS

15 to 20 x 3 mm Fire Polished beads – Copper Lined Crystal

GENERAL INSTRUCTIONS

- Stretch the fabric print over 16" x 12" stretcher bars. The original was worked on Edmunds stretcher bars.
- Make sure that the print is taut. This will improve the quality of your work.
- Assume that threads are stranded cotton unless otherwise described.
- If you are unsure of any of the stitches, practise on a scrap of fabric before working on the project.
- When working with stranded cotton, use two strands in a size 7 embroidery needle, unless otherwise advised.
- If advised to use a single strand, work with a size 10 embroidery needle.
- Work with a single strand, doubled over and threaded onto a size 11 sharps quilting needle for all bead embroidery stitches.
- Work with a long beading needle and beading thread when constructing the three-dimensional beaded elements.
- Work with a single strand of Perle and Dentelles threads.
- Use a size 7 embroidery needle when you work the warp stitches in the weaving.
- Use a size 26 tapestry needle for the weaving weft stitches and the needle-lace detached button-hole stitches.

STITCHING INSTRUCTIONS

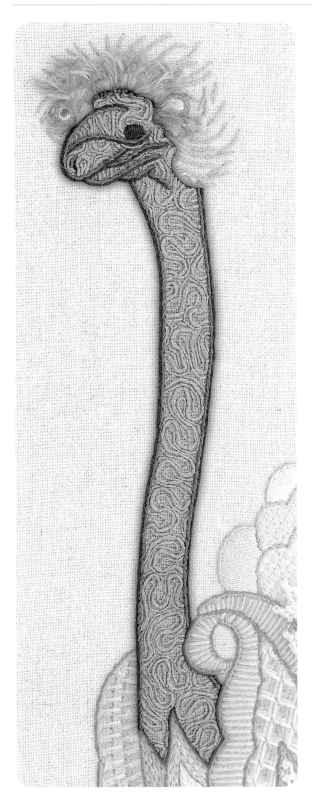

1. Using a blue tailor's washout pen, accentuate the lines of the face so that they will show through the vermicelli couching.

2. Using a single strand of 3781, pad the nostril with horizontal satin stitch.

3. Using the same thread, work vertical satin stitch over the padding.

4. Using 3782, fill the neck of the ostrich with the two-thread variation of Vermicelli couching found in the embroidery stitches gallery.

5. Using the colour image as your guide, work over the lines of the face, continuing up to what will be the start of the 'hair line' towards the top of the head.

6. Using two strands of 3790, work whipped backstitch over the lines of the face and down each side of the neck.

7. Using a single strand of 3781, work outline stitch on one side of the whipped backstitch. In the lower half of the face it should be below the whipped backstitch. As you work around the lines, it will be on the upper side at the top of the face.

8. With the same thread and when you have completed the surrounding embroidery at the bottom of the neck, work outline stitch on the outside edge of the whipped backstitch that outlines each side of the neck.

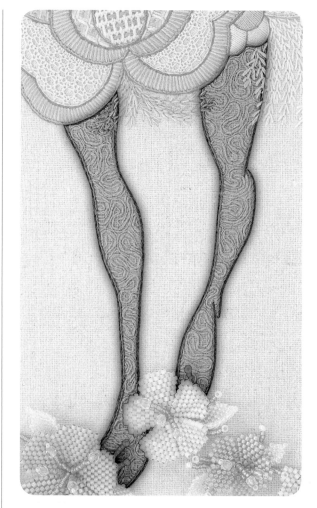

9. With a single strand of 3790, couch two strands of the same thread over each of the lines that make up the rest of the face and head.

10. Following the instructions for caged flat-back crystals on page 60 – working directly onto fabric – of the bead embroidery gallery, attach a 20ss Smoke Topaz AB flat-back crystal on the circle provided for each eye, using a single strand of 3781.

11. Thread a single strand each of 3790 and 3781 onto a size 7 embroidery needle and following the instructions for 'bad hair day' tufting on page 29, use the colour image as your guide to determine the direction in which the loops should lie.

12. With this stitch, work moth-eaten feathers at the base of the crown, around the bottom of each eye and, also, on the inside sections that surround the eye.

13. Using the colour image as your guide, trim the tufting. You want to be a little careless with this so that the face of the ostrich looks slightly comical – which is exactly how it looks in real life.

14. Using 3782, fill the legs of the ostrich with the two-thread variation of Vermicelli couching.

15. Ostriches have very ugly feet and I have chosen to cover them up with three-dimensional beaded flowers, the guidelines for which appear later in these instructions. For now, finish the stitching for the feet knowing that they will be hidden.

16. Using two strands of 3790, work whipped back-stitch over the outside lines of each leg.

17. Using a single strand of 3781, work outline stitch on the outer side of the whipped backstitch.

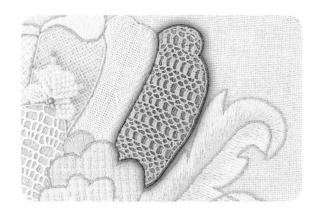

18. Moving to the tail feathers, fill this portion with vertical long and short stitch using a single strand of 3782.

19. Using Dentelles Ecru, work backstitch around the top and right side.

20. Following the instructions for needle-lace filler 1 on page 65, work over the background stitching from the tip to the base.

21. When you reach the base, attach it to the fabric by coming up through the fabric, working through the loop in the previous row, going back into the fabric and coming up in line with the next loop in the previous row, ready to work through that one.

22. With the same thread, whip the backstitch edge.

23. When you have completed the leaf shape on the right, outline the whipped backstitch with a single strand of 3790.

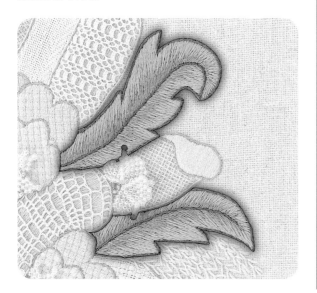

24. Fill these sections with diagonal long and short stitch shading, starting with a single strand of 3782 adjacent to the vein, shading out to 3033 on the outer edges on each side.

25. Using a single strand of 3790, work outline stitch down the vein to hide the raw edges of the shading stitches.

26. When you have completed the embroidery that surrounds these sections, define the edges with outline stitch using a single strand of 3790.

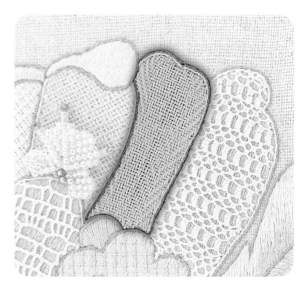

27. Working the warp stitches over the shortest length, fill this shape with needle-weaving texture no. 6 on page 71, using Dentelles Ecru for colour 1 and Dentelles 3033 for colour 2.

28. Using Dentelles Ecru, work whipped backstitch around the top and the right side of the shape.

29. Work outline stitch on the outer edge of the whipped backstitch using a single strand of 3790.

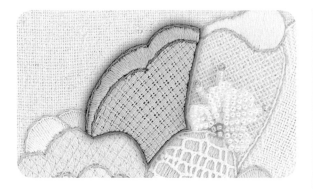

30. Working the warp stitches from tip to base, fill this section with needle weaving texture no. 8 on page 72, using Dentelles Ecru for colours 1 and 2.

31. Using two strands of 644, pad the top section with stem stitch.

32. With a single strand of the same thread, work vertical satin stitch over the padding, fanning around to suit the shape.

33. Define the top and bottom edges with outline stitch using a single strand of 3790.

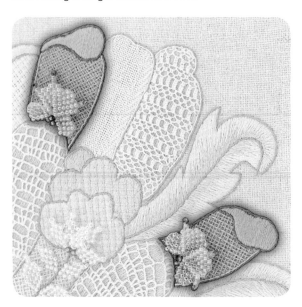

34. Work both sections in the same way.

35. Fill the bottom part of the shape with woven trellis couching following the guidelines on page 28. Use a single strand of 3033 for shade 1, the trellis, 3782 for shade 2, the couching, and 644 for shades 3 and 4, the weaving.

36. Using Dentelles Ecru, work whipped backstitch on both sides of the woven trellis in the case of the shape depicted on the left in the image above and on the right-hand edge of the image on the right.

37. Define the outside edge of the whipped backstitch with outline stitch using a single strand of 3790.

38. Using two strands of 3033 for the shape depicted on the left in the image above and 644 for the shape on the right, pad the top section with stem stitch.

39. With a single strand of the same thread, work vertical satin stitch over the padding, fanning around to suit the shape.

40. Work outline stitch around the padded satin stitch using a single strand of 3790.

TIP

Whether you make the three-dimensional elements now or later, it is a good idea to only attach them to the fabric when you have completed the embroidery because once they are in place, every single stitch you do will involve the thread catching on the beaded flowers or leaves. This applies to all the beaded flowers and leaves in this design.

41. Referring to the three-dimensional beaded elements on page 54, work a six- to eight-bead combination flower for the bottom of each of these shapes.

42. Use beads 15° 2442 and cream beading thread.

43. Attach each flower with the tails of working thread stitching three beads 15° 650 in the space where the petals meet at the bottom.

44. Before you end off the working thread and referring to the general instructions on pages 32 to 34, work three beaded twigs that come out from behind the petals.

45. Use between five and seven beads 15° 1527 and a single bead 15° 650 at the tip.

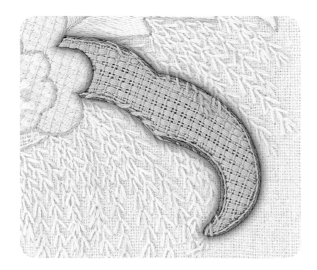

46. Working the warp stitches from edge to edge, fill this section with needle weaving texture no. 8 on page 72, using Dentelles Ecru for colours 1 and 2.

47. Using the same thread, work whipped backstitch around the outer edge.

48. Using a single strand of 3790, work outline stitch on the outside of the whipped backstitch.

49. Work fly stitch on each of the lines that depict the down feathers.

50. Thread a needle with a single thread each of 644 and 3033.

51. Thread a second needle with a single thread each of 644 and 3782.

52. Work rows of fly stitch, varying and alternating the use of these two needles as you go along and, where appropriate, stitching over the woven tail feather at the back and over the top of the leg at the front.

53. Moving forward to the front row of tail feathers, these two areas are worked in the same way.

54. It will be easiest for you to turn the work around so that you are working upside down.

55. Fill each shape with long and short stitch using a single strand of 3782.

56. Using Dentelles Ecru, work backstitch around the shape, leaving out the indentations made by the petals from the adjacent shapes.

57. Referring to the needle-lace techniques gallery, work stitch no. 26 (variation) on page 64, from the base to the tip of the shape using Dentelles Ecru.

58. Using the same thread, whip the available backstitch that is around the shape.

59. When you have completed the surrounding embroidery, using a single strand of 3790, work outline stitch on the outside of the whipped backstitch.

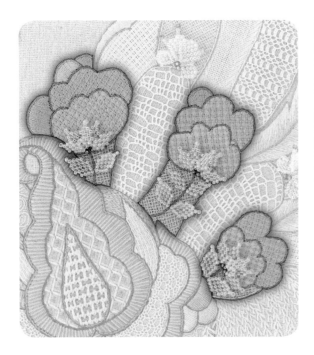

60. Work these sections in the same way.

61. Using a blue washout pen, go over the line of the stem in the bottom part so that you will be able to see it through the woven trellis.

62. Fill the bottom part of the shape with woven trellis couching. Use a single strand of 3033 for shade 1, the trellis, 3782 for shade 2, the couching, and 644 for shades 3 and 4, the weaving.

63. Using two strands of 3790, work a line of whipped backstitch over the woven trellis along the line of the stem which you should be able to see peeping through the trellis.

64. Moving to the flower above the area you have just worked, fill the bottom shape with horizontal satin stitch using two strands of 3033.

65. With a single strand of the same thread, work vertical long and short stitch over the padding.

66. Fill the top shape with vertical long and short stitching using a single strand of 644.

67. Using the colour image above as your guide, work basic trellis couching over both shapes at the same time with a single strand of 3782.

68. When you have completed the surrounding embroidery, define each section of the flower with outline stitch using a single strand of 3790.

69. Adjacent to the left side highlighted section are three semi-circles. There is also one adjacent to the middle section.

70. Using the stipulated threads, pad the semi-circle with horizontal satin stitch using two strands of cotton.

71. Using a single strand of the same thread, work vertical buttonhole stitch over the padding, fanning it slightly as you work around the shape.

72. Use the following threads for those adjacent to the left side shape:

- Large bottom left – 3782
- Medium top centre – 3033
- Small top right – 3782
- The shape adjacent to the centre section is worked with 3782.

73. Define the top edge of each semi-circle by working outline stitch adjacent to the ridge on the outside of the buttonhole stitch using a single strand of 3790.

74. Referring to the Three-dimensional beaded elements on page 32, work an eight-bead calyx for each of the 3 sections.

75. With cream beading thread, use beads 15° 1527 for the first and last leaf shapes and 15° 2442 for the three centre shapes.

76. With cream beading thread and beads 15° 1527 work the following leaves, attaching them to each side of the whipped backstitch stem:

- Left section – one pair 10-bead leaves;
- Middle section – one pair 10-bead leaves at the bottom; one pair eight-bead leaves at the top;
- Right side section – one pair 10-bead leaves.

77. Using the colour image as your guide, attach each element with the tails of working threads.

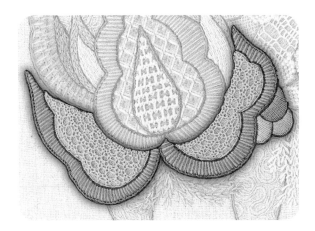

78. Work both shapes in the same way.

79. Fill the centre of the shape with vertical long and short stitch using a single strand of 3033.

80. Using Dentelles 3033, work back stitch all the way around the long and short stitched area.

81. Referring to the instructions for needle-lace edging no. 9 on page 64, work needle lace over the long and short stitch starting at the base of the petal and working out towards the edge on each side.

82. Using the same thread, whip the backstitch that surrounds the needle lace.

83. Using two strands of 3782, pad the outer edge of each shape with closely packed rows of stem stitch.

84. Following the instructions for striped blanket stitch on page 18, work blanket stitch over the padding with the ridge facing to the outer edge, fanning the stitching slightly as necessary.

85. Use two strands of 3790 for the blanket stitch and 3782 for the straight stitches.

86. When you have completed the surrounding embroidery, work outline stitch adjacent to the outer edge of the ridge, continuing down the side of the shapes where they taper off at the top. Use a single strand of 3781.

87. With the same thread, work outline stitch over the backstitch in the ditch between the needle lace and the striped blanket stitch.

88. Work the semi-circles on the right of the right-side shape in the same way as those you have already done, with padded buttonhole stitch using threads as under:

- Top centre – 3032
- Bottom left – 644
- Bottom right – 3782.

89. Define the outside edge of each semi-circle by working outline stitch adjacent to the ridge on the outside of the buttonhole stitch using a single strand of 3790.

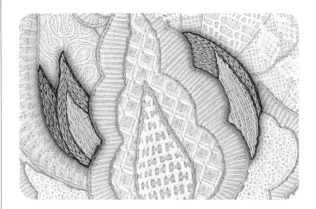

90. Starting on the left, fill the shape with vertical chain stitch backstitch combination using two strands of 3790 for the chain stitch, a single strand of 3782 for the backstitch.

91. Moving right, work raised stem stitch in the centre shape. Work a row with two strands of 3033, followed by a row with two strands of 3782, thereafter alternating the colours.

92. Fill the outer edge with a row of vertical chain stitch backstitch combination, meeting at the tip. Use two strands of 3032 for the chain stitch, a single strand of 3033 for the backstitch.

93. When you have completed the surrounding embroidery, define each shape, including the centre, with outline stitch using a single strand of 3781.

94. Moving over to the other side, fill the bottom shape with two-colour raised stem stitch using the 3033/3782 colour combination.

95. Fill the top shape with rows of chain stitch backstitch combination using strands of 3032 for the chain stitch a single strand of 3033 for the backstitch.

96. When you have completed the surrounding embroidery, define each shape with outline stitch using a single strand of 3781.

97. Starting on the inner edge of this shape, adjacent to the neck, fill this area with layered buttonhole stitch.

98. Using the lines on the drawing as your guide, work the first row using two strands of 3790.

99. Follow this with a row worked with two strands of 3032 and then a row worked with two strands of 3033.

100. Work a fourth row, immediately outside the third row, with the ridge touching the ridge of the third row. Use two strands of 3790.

101. Define the outer edge with outline stitch worked with a single strand of 3781.

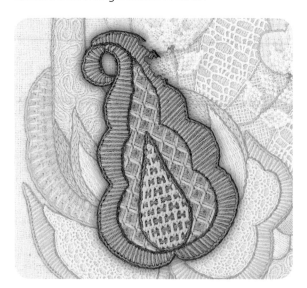

102. The easiest sequence of work for this shape is to begin by working the middle area, as opposed to the centre.

103. Fill this area with battlement couching using two strands each of 3032 for the first layer, 3782 for the second and 3033 for the top, lightest layer of stitches.

104. Work the small straight couching stitch with a single strand of 3790.

105. With two strands of 3790, place a single wrap French knot in the centre of the remaining space.

106. Moving to the centre of this shape, fill it with woven raised chain stitch. Use three strands of 3033 for the raised chain stitch and three strands of 3790 for the weaving.

107. Outline this area with whipped back stitch using two strands of 3790.

108. Define the outer edge with outline stitch using a single strand of 3781.

109. Moving now to the outside edge of this shape, pad each of the sections with stem stitching using two strands of 3782.

110. Following the instructions for striped blanket stitch on page 18, work blanket stitch over the padding with the ridge facing to the outer edge, fanning the stitching slightly as necessary and using the colour image as your guide.

111. Use two strands of 3790 for the blanket stitch and 3782 for the straight stitches.

112. When you have completed the surrounding embroidery, work outline stitch adjacent to the outer edge of the ridge, all the way around. Use a single strand of 3781.

113. With the same thread, work outline stitch in the ditch between the battlement couching and the striped blanket stitch.

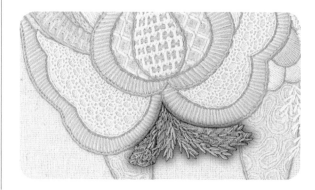

114. Work fly stitch on each of the lines that depict these finer feathers.

115. Thread a needle with a single thread each of 3790 and 3782.

116. Thread a second needle with a single thread each of 3032 and 3782.

117. Work rows of fly stitch, varying and alternating the use of these two needles as you go along and, where appropriate, stitching over the tops of the legs.

And now it is time to have fun making the three-dimensional beaded flowers to hide those ugly feet. The table below lists the flowers and accompanying leaves that you will need to make.

Delica bead size 11	Superlon beading thread size AA	Flower sizes	Flower stamens: stalks bead 15° 650; tips 1 x 3 mm fire polished bead copper lined crystal with stopper bead 15° 2442	Accompanying leaves: bead 15° 1527 and cream beading thread
1451	Cream	1 x 6-bead flower	1 stamen with 3-bead stalk	1 x 8-bead leaf 1 x 10-bead leaf
		1 x 8-bead flower	3 stamens with 4- to 6-bead stalks	1 x 8-bead leaf 1 x 12-bead leaf
		1 x 10-bead flower	3 stamens with 4- to 6-bead stalks	1 x 16-bead leaf
1459	Ash	1 x 12-bead flower	5 stamens with 5- to 8-bead stalks	2 x 16-bead leaves 1 x 14-bead leaf
1731	Ash	1 x 8-bead flower	3 stamens with 4- to 6-bead stalks	1 x 10-bead leaf 1 x 12-bead leaf

118. Refer to the instructions for attaching flowers and leaves to the fabric on page 34.

119. As you attach each flower, use the thread tails to make little twigs that come out from underneath the petals and soften the effect. The stalks of the twigs are made up with beads 15° 650 and you should pick up as many beads as you need to accommodate the length of the stalk.

120. At the tip of each stalk is a single bead 11° 577.

121. Work from the left and using the colour image above as your guide, attach the flowers as follows:

- Cream six-bead flower: eight-bead leaf radiating from bottom left with a 10-bead leaf slightly below that.

- Shell pink 12-bead flower: placement of leaves evenly spaced, radiating out in three places with the two 16-bead leaves in the bottom half and the 14-bead leaf, at top left.

- Cream 10-bead flower: 16-bead leaf radiating from side upper left.

- Beige eight-bead flower: 10-bead leaf radiating from upper right side. 12-bead leaf radiating from bottom right.

- Cream six-bead flower: eight-bead leaf radiating from upper right side with a 10-bead leaf slightly below that.

Maureen

OWL

Dimensions: 560 x 340 mm (22 x 13$\frac{3}{8}$")

Owls are found on every continent, except Antarctica, and being one of the oldest species of vertebrate animals in existence, have featured significantly in world folklore. Many believe the owl to be a bad omen whereas others believe it to be a symbol for good. Whatever you believe, it is an interesting bird and certainly a fine subject for an embroidery project. This owl is a big girl and whilst probably not for the faint-hearted, comprises a wide variety of stitches and techniques. When framed, it will find pride of place on any wall.

Materials

FABRIC

750 x 550 mm (29½ x 21½") natural coloured cotton linen blend base fabric
750 x 550 mm (29½ x 21½") off-white cotton voile backing fabric

EMBROIDERY FRAME

14" embroidery hoop
Scroll frame with 36" cross bars

NEEDLES

Size 7 Embroidery needles
Size 10 Embroidery needles
Size 11 Sharps quilting needles
Size 12 Long beading needles
Size 26 Tapestry needles
Size 24 Tapestry needles

THREADS AND BEADS

DMC STRANDED COTTON

ECRU	Ecru
152	Medium Light Shell Pink
155	Blue Violet
221	Very Dark Shell Pink
224	Very Light Shell Pink
350	Medium Coral
422	Light Hazelnut Brown
543	Ultra Very Light Beige Brown
746	Off White
838	Very Dark Beige Brown
839	Dark Beige Brown x 2
840	Medium Beige Brown x 2
841	Light Beige Brown x 2
842	Very Light Beige Brown
869	Very Dark Hazelnut Brown
975	Dark Golden Brown
976	Medium Golden Brown
3011	Dark Khaki Green
3012	Medium Khaki Green
3013	Light Khaki Green
3051	Dark Green Grey
3052	Medium Green Grey
3053	Green Grey
3721	Dark Shell Pink
3746	Dark Blue Violet
3782	Light Mocha Brown
3823	Ultra Pale Yellow
3826	Golden Brown
3827	Pale Golden Brown
3828	Hazelnut Brown
3854	Medium Autumn Gold
3855	Light Autumn Gold
3857	Dark Rosewood
3858	Medium Rosewood
3859	Light Rosewood

DMC COLOUR VARIATIONS STRANDED COTTON

4090	Golden Oasis
4110	Sunrise
4120	Tropical Sunset
4145	Sand Dune
4160	Glistening Pearl
4220	Lavender Fields

DMC PERLE #12

ECRU	Ecru x 2
223	Light Shell Pink
224	Very Light Shell Pink
842	Very Light Beige Brown

DMC DENTELLES #80

ECRU	Ecru

LIZBETH #40

693	Medium Linen

DI VAN NIEKERK HAND-PAINTED SILK RIBBON

4 mm	110	Wheat
2 mm	110	Wheat

SUPERLON BEADING THREAD AA

Cream
Olive

MIYUKI BEADS
Size 15°

2g	132FR	Matte Transparent Light Topaz AB
4g	650	Rustic Gray Silver Lined Alabaster
2g	1421	SL Golden Olive
4g	1883	Transparent Wine Gold Luster

Size 15° Delica (DBS)

4g	124	Transparent Golden Olive Luster
4g	203	Cream Ceylon

PRECIOSA VIVA 12 FLAT-BACK CRYSTALS
2 pieces   34ss Smoke Topaz AB

GENERAL INSTRUCTIONS

- Make sure that the print is taut in the hoop or frame. This will improve the quality of your work.
- Assume that threads are stranded cotton unless otherwise described.
- If you are unsure of any of the stitches, practise on a scrap of fabric before working on the project.
- When working with stranded cotton, use two strands in a size 7 embroidery needle, unless otherwise advised.
- If advised to use a single strand, work with a size 10 embroidery needle.
- Work with a single strand, doubled over and threaded onto a size 11 sharps quilting or a size 12 bead embroidery needle for all bead embroidery stitches.
- Work with a long beading needle and a single strand of beading thread when constructing the three-dimensional beaded elements.
- Work with a single strand of Perle and Dentelles threads.
- Use a size 7 embroidery needle when you work the warp stitches in the weaving.
- Use a size 24 tapestry needle for the weaving weft stitches and a size 26 tapestry needle for the needle-lace detached buttonhole stitches.

STITCHING INSTRUCTIONS

- Because of its size, you will find it easier to work this project in two different hoops and frames.
- Without adding any beads, work each section in a 14" hoop, moving it around and re-stretching it in the hoop as each exposed area is stitched.
- When you have completed all the embroidery, stretch it in a frame that accommodates the entire project – I used a scroll frame with 36" cross bars – to attach the beads and beaded elements.

TIP

When needle weaving, I normally advise that you always go back to the same side to start each weft row so that the pattern is not lost. The woven areas in this project are large and, as a result, you end up with very long strands of thread at the back of the work. It is for this reason that I have deliberately chosen weaving patterns that make it easy to go backwards and forwards, using the illustration in the weaving pattern to guide you. The threads used have been calculated using this method.

1. Starting in the centre of the middle tail feather, work needle weaving stitch, texture no. 5 on page 71. Turn the work sideways, placing the warp stitches down the shortest side and the weft stitches along the length of the feather.

2. When you work the other side, turn it sideways the other way so that you get a mirror image of the first side, in this way giving the look of a feather with the diagonal impression going downwards and out-wards on either side.

3. Use Perle #12 842 for the warp and Perle #12 Ecru for the weft stitches.

4. With a single strand of 840 on a tapestry needle and using the image below left as your guide, weave over and under the weft stitches after every second diagonal line created by the lighter warp stitches. This accentuates the lines rather well.

5. With the same thread, whip the warp stitch that creates the central line of the feather.

6. With a doubled-over strand of the same thread on a bead embroidery needle, attach a single bead 15° 650 over the central weft stitch at evenly spaced intervals. Bring your needle up on one side of the whipped weft stitch and take it back into the fabric on the other side of the stitch, continuing until you reach the lowest line that has been woven with the single strand of 840.

7. When you have completed the surrounding embroidery, using a single strand of 839, work outline stitch around the tail feather.

8. Using a single strand of the same thread, work single-wrap French knots at small, regular intervals, adjacent to the outside of the outline stitch.

9. Moving outwards, the tail feathers on either side of the central feather are worked in the same way.

10. Referring to trellis with cross-stitch couching variation 1 on page 28, work a trellis over the entire feather using two strands of Ecru.

11. Work a cross stitch over each intersection using two strands of 3053.

12. Using two strands of 152, work sheaf stitch (or part sheaf stitch) in the centre of each block that has been formed by the trellis couching.

13. Using a single strand of 839, work outline stitch around the bottom of the tail feather.

14. Using a single strand of same thread, work single-wrap French knots at small, regular intervals, adjacent to the outside of the outline stitch.

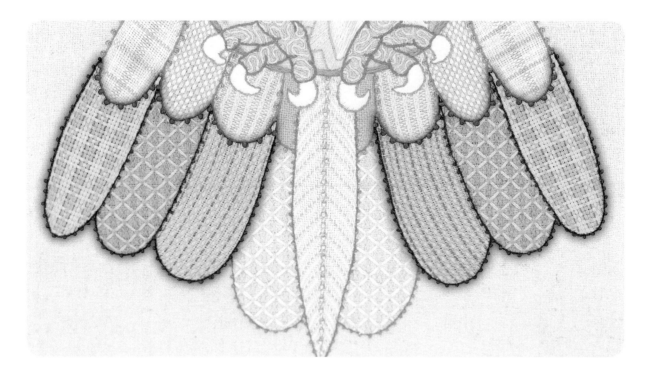

15. Working out from the centre, fill the next tail feather on each side with needle-weaving texture no. 3 on page 71.

16. Turn the frame sideways and work the warp stitches across the short side using colour 1, Perle #12 842.

17. Work the weft stitches using colour 1, Perle #12 842 and colour 2, Perle #12 Ecru.

18. When you have completed the weaving, weave a single strand of stranded cotton 840 between rows 1 and 2, following the pattern of row 1.

19. Moving outwards to the next tail feather and referring to trellis with cross-stitch couching variation 1 on page 28, work a trellis over the entire feather using two strands of Ecru.

20. Work a cross stitch over each intersection using two strands of 3053.

21. Using two strands of 152, work sheaf stitch (or part sheaf stitch) in the centre of each block that has been formed by the trellis couching.

22. Moving outwards, fill the outside tail feather with weaving stitch checks and stripes no. 9 on page 69, using Perle #12 842 for colour 1 and Perle #12 Ecru for colour 2. Turn the frame sideways and work the warp stitches across the short side.

23. When you have completed the weaving, weave a single strand of stranded cotton 840 on each side of the darker stripe that has formed, following the pattern of the darker row on each side.

24. Using the colour image above as your guide, and working with a single strand of 839, work outline stitch around the bottom and sides of the tail feathers as needed.

25. Using a single strand of the same thread, work single-wrap French knots at small, regular intervals, adjacent to the outside of the outline stitch.

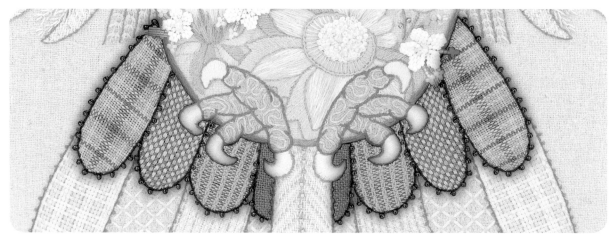

26. Moving up a step and, once again, working from the centre outwards, fill the inside feathers on each side with basic single weaving using Perle #12 223.

27. Moving outwards, the feather on either side of the single weaving is filled with weaving checks and stripes no. 6 (*see* page 69). Use Perle #12 224 for colour 1 and 223 for colour 2, working the weft stitches over the shortest side.

28. The next feather on either side is filled with weaving checks and stripes no. 13 (*see* page 70) using Perle #12 223 for colour 1, 224 for colour 2 and Ecru for colour 3.

29. Fill the outside tail feather on either side with hecks and stripes tartan variation (*see* page 70). Work the warp stitches over the shortest side, starting in the middle of the space and working to either side following a colour sequence identical to the rows as listed.

30. Use Perle #12 223 for colour 1, Ecru for colour 2, 842 for colour 3 and 224 for colour 4.

31. Starting in the middle of the space with row 1, work the weft stitches following the colour sequence out to either side.

32. Using the colour image above as your guide and, working with a single strand of 221, work outline stitch around the bottom and sides of the tail feathers as needed.

33. When any surrounding embroidery is complete and using a doubled-over single strand of the same thread, attach a single bead 15° 1883 at regular intervals, adjacent to the outside of the outline stitch.

34. Moving to the flowers inside the tummy and starting with the flower coming out from behind the claws, fill the centre of each outward facing leaf, as well as the five petals at the top of the flower, with long and short stitch using a single strand of colour variations 4220.

TIP

When working with multi-coloured or variegated thread you are in danger of ending up with blocks of colour, which are not ideal. The solution to this problem is to spread each colour over the space before it morphs into the next colour. Refer to the instructions for long and short stitch worked with colour variations on page 24.

35. Pad the outside border of each leaf with lines of stem stitch using two strands of thread.

36. Work diagonal satin stitch over the padding using a single strand of thread.

37. Use 3013 for the leaves that radiate from the front of the flower and 3012 for those towards the back.

38. Outline the outside edge of the border with outline stitch using a single strand of 3011.

39. Work a line of outline stitch in the ditch between the coloured centre of each leaf and the outside border. Use a single strand of 3746.

40. Using the same thread, define each of the petals at the top of the flower with outline stitch.

41. Moving to the centre of the blue flower, work a line of double blanket stitch around the perimeter, starting with the outward facing line which uses two strands of 155.

42. Moving to the inward facing row, use two strands of 4220.

43. Using a single strand of 3746, define the outer edge with outline stitch worked adjacent to the ridge of the blanket stitch.

44. Combine a single strand each of 3823 and colour variations 4090 on the needle and fill the centre of the flower with a layer of two-wrap French knots.

45. Work a second layer in a smaller circle forming the central area of the shape to create perspective.

46. Using a doubled-over strand of 3823, stitch single beads 15° 132FR at evenly spaced intervals between the knots.

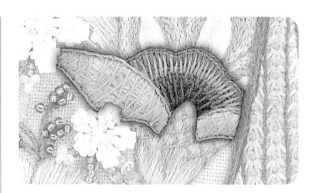

47. Moving to the flower on the top right of the tummy, these instructions also apply to the golden-brown flower that features in the floral section of each wing.

48. Referring to the highlighted areas in the image above, work layered buttonhole stitch in the centre of the flower.

49. Start at the base using a single strand of 975, moving through to 3826 for the second row.

50. Because the stitches fan out to accommodate the widening of the shape, work two buttonhole stitches into each gap in the next row using 976.

51. Starting at the top edge of the shape and using 3827, do a single buttonhole stitch into each gap when working the next row.

52. Placing the ridge of the final row immediately above the ridge of the previous row, finish up using 976 again.

53. Using two strands of 3782, work horizontal satin stitch padding on each of the petals – one full and one half visible – that radiate out on either side of the flower.

TIP

Padding is usually worked with the same colour thread of the stitch that will be worked over the padding. If, however, the overlying stitch will be worked in varying colours, it is a good idea to work the padding in thread that is as close as possible to the colour of the base fabric.

54. Using a single strand of 4090 and following the suggested method for using colour variations thread in the stitch guide, work vertical long and short stitch over the padding.

55. Using a single strand of 3827, work back stitches around each side of each petal.

56. Following the guidelines in the stitch gallery and using the same thread, work interlaced herringbone stitch over each petal.

57. Still using the same thread, whip the backstitch on the top and bottom of each petal.

58. Pad the calyx at the bottom with horizontal satin stitch using two strands of 3782.

59. Work vertical long and short stitch shading over the padding, starting at the base with a single strand of 3827 shading through 3052 to 3053 at the tip.

60. Using the image above to guide you, work intermittent trellis couching in the top half of the calyx using a single strand of 3051.

61. Using the same thread, work outline stitch around the entire calyx.

62. Moving to the top of the flower, fill the small petals with vertical long and short stitch. Start at the base with a single strand of 976, shading through to 3827 at the tip.

63. Pad the centre of the big leaves with horizontal satin stitch using two strands of 3782.

64. Work vertical satin stitch over the padding using a single strand of 4090.

65. Using a single strand of 3012, work two rows of chain stitch adjacent to and around the centre of the leaf.

66. Using a single strand of 3013, work a row of chain stitch along the outside line of the leaf.

67. With the same thread, fill in the remaining space with rows and part rows of chain stitch.

68. With a single strand of 3011, define the outside of the leaf with outline stitch.

69. With the same thread, work a line of outline stitch in the ditch between the centre of the leaf and the first row of chain stitch.

70. The stem leading up to the base of the flower, along with the stems that hold the small buds, are done with backstitch worked with two strands of 3011.

71. Whip the backstitch with a single strand of the same thread.

72. To spread the colour, take two strands of colour variations 4120, pull them apart and change the direction of the one strand by marrying the end of it with the beginning of the other.

73. Referring to the instructions for multiple wrap French knots on page 23 and starting at the tip of the stem, work a three-wrap French knot. Thereafter work two pairs of knots, one each side of the stem,

increasing by a wrap for each pair with finally a single knot at the bottom that has six wraps. Start that knot on one side of the stem and complete it on the other, so that it sits in the centre of the bud.

74. Moving on to the beaded flowers, it is advisable to only attach them right at the end of the project.

75. Referring to the three-dimensional elements in the bead embroidery gallery on page 32 and making sure that you have read the general instructions at the beginning of that chapter, work the flower on the lower right section of the image alongside left as a six-bead flower with cream beading thread and beads 15° Delica 203. It is placed on the small dot provided in the drawing.

76. The leaf coming out of the bottom of the flower is an eight-bead leaf worked with olive beading thread and beads 15° Delica 124.

77. When you have attached the flower, come up in the centre of the flower, pick up three 15° 132FR beads and go back into the fabric in the same place thereby creating a small loop of yellow.

78. Soften this small arrangement with about three twigs radiating out from under the flower using three to five beads 15° 650 for the stems and three 15° 132FR beads at the tips.

79. The smaller flower above the one you have just done is a four-bead flower. It is placed on the small dot provided in the drawing and has two radiating twigs. These elements are worked with the same beads and beading threads.

80. These instructions describing the bullion knot buds refer to all the buds that appear in the tummy section, as well as those that are in the floral section of each wing.

81. Using two strands of 3051, work the short stem with whipped backstitch.

82. Using two strands of 4220, create the buds with four- to six-wrap bullions, starting at the tip and working down the stem. When working the two pairs adjacent to the stem, make sure that you keep the angles sharp.

83. Moving up slightly to the right, using two strands of 3051, work the leaf stems with whipped backstitch.

84. Using the same thread and following the guidelines in the bead embroidery gallery, work an eight-bead beaded lazy daisy (*see page 59*) on the tip of each stem. Use beads 15° 1421.

85. Stitch a single bead 15° 1421 adjacent to each side of the longer stem using the colour image as your guide.

86. Above and to the right of the leaves is a four-bead flower with two stamens radiating out of the top of it. Use the same beads and threads used for the other flowers and only attach it once you have done the surrounding embroidery.

87. Moving to the flower at the top of the tummy, fill the middle of the main part with long and short stitch shading. Use a single strand of colour variations 4110, following the guidelines for long and short stitch worked with colour variations on page 24.

88. Fill the outer portion with long and short stitch using a single strand of 3859.

89. Using a single strand of 3858, work basic trellis couching over the long and short stitch.

90. Using the same thread, work outline stitch in the ditch between the two sections of the bloom.

91. When you have completed the surrounding embroidery, and using the same thread, define the outside section with outline stitch.

92. Fill each ovate shape with raised herringbone stitch. Use a single strand of 3053 for the green leaves and a single strand of 4110 for the coloured petals.

93. Work the stems at the base of the bloom with whipped backstitch using two strands of 3051.

94. Referring to the colour image above, work a six-bead beaded lazy daisy on the tip of each stem. Use beads 15° 1421.

95. Stitch a single bead 15° 1421 adjacent to each side of the longer stem using the colour image as your guide.

96. Above and to the right of the bloom is a six-bead flower with an eight-bead and a 10-bead leaf radiating out of the top left. There is a single stamen around those leaves and two stamens coming out of the bottom of the flower. Use the same beads and threads you used for the other elements and only attach them once you have done the surrounding embroidery.

97. Moving to the flower on the left of the owl's tummy, these instructions also apply to the coral-yellow flower that features in the floral section of each wing.

98. Fill each of the petals highlighted in the image above with long and short stitch shading using a single strand of colour variations 4120. Follow the guidelines for working long and short stitch with colour variations.

99. Using a single strand of 350, work intermittent outline stitch around each petal to highlight shade and shadow on the edges and to suggest division between the petals.

100. Moving to the leaves, or petals if you will, at the bottom of the flower and using the image above as your guide, fill one side of each shape with diagonal satin stitch using a single strand of 4120.

101. The remaining side of each shape is filled with green diagonal satin stitch. Use a single strand of 3052 for the bottom, centre shapes and a single strand of 3053 for each of the side leaves.

102. Using two strands of 3782, work horizontal satin stitch padding over the shape that forms the calyx.

103. With a single strand of each thread, work vertical long and short stitch shading over the padding. Start at the base with 3854 shading through 3855 to 3823 at the tip.

104. Define the calyx with outline stitch using a single strand of 976.

105. The leaves that lay over the calyx are worked with long double detached chain stitches. Use two strands of thread and using the image above as your guide, work some with 3052 and others with 3051.

106. Using the same threads and beads as before and going clockwise from the top the details for the flowers and leaves in the image above are as follows:
- four-bead flower, eight-bead leaf, two stamens;
- six-bead flower, two 10- and one eight-bead leaves, five stamens;
- six-bead flower, eight-bead leaf, three stamens;
- four-bead flower, eight-bead leaf, two stamens.

107. Moving back to the top, work the stems with whipped backstitch using two strands of 3051.

108. Work the bullion knot buds as described earlier using two strands of 4220.

109. Work eight-bead beaded lazy daisy leaves using beads 15° 1421 and thread 3051.

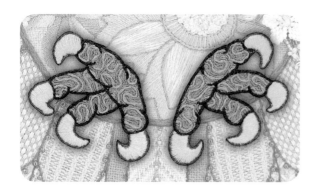

110. Following the guidelines for vermicelli couching and the two-thread variation on page 30, fill the owl's toes. Work the stitch continuously as you will define each toe later.

111. Use two strands of 422 couched down with a single strand of the same thread for the first sequence.

112. The second sequence is worked in single strands of 3828.

113. Using two strands of 746, pad each claw with stem stitch that runs along the length of the talon.

114. Using a single strand of the same thread, work satin stitch over the padding. Work over the shortest distance, at right angles to the padding and fanning the satin stitch as you follow the shape of the claw.

115. Define each toe with whipped backstitch using two strands of 838.

116. Define the remaining sides of each claw with outline stitch using a single strand of 869.

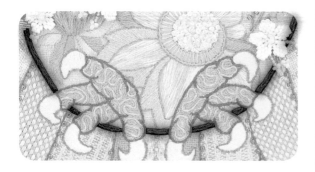

117. When you have completed the wings, outline the sides and bottom of the tummy, starting at the top and swinging around, going between the claws and finishing at the top on the other side with heavy chain stitch. Use two strands of 3858.

118. Because the line is broken up it is difficult to achieve the impression of an unbroken consistent line. To this end, work a row of outline stitch with a single strand of 3857 on the outside edge of the heavy chain stitch.

The wings of the owl are identical. The following instructions are for the wing on the right. The wing on the left is worked in the same way but will be a mirror image of what you do for the right-side wing.

119. Referring to the image above, starting on the section adjacent to the body, work a line of wheatear stitch on each of the lines depicted in the line drawing, except for the last line on the right.

120. Use two strands of colour variations 4110. Working from tip to base and starting with the longest line, try to make sure that the side stitches of the wheatear stitch go in and out of the same holes as those in the previous line.

121. Using two strands of 3859, work a two-wrap French knot into the centre of each petal shape that has formed in the wheatear stitch.

122. Using a single strand of 3858, work whipped backstitch up the line that you missed on the right.

123. Using the same thread, work a line of whipped backstitch between the lines of wheatear, working over the point where the side stitches intersect.

124. Placing the warp stitches over the shortest side – as you will with all the feathers – fill the adjacent feather with needle weaving stitch, texture no. 5 (*see* page 71). Use Perle #12 842 for the warp and Perle #12 Ecru for the weft stitches. The lines on the drawing are there to give you the direction of both the warp and weft stitches. They are merely a guide and you will cover them with the needle weaving.

125. With a single strand of 840 on a tapestry needle and using the image above as your guide, weave over and under the weft stitches after every second diagonal line created by the lighter warp stitches.

126. Using the colour image above as your guide, outline the right-hand side and half of the left-hand side of this wing feather with outline stitch using a single strand of 839.

127. Move on to the feather that is in the middle of the image above.

128. Using Perle #12 Ecru for colour 1 and 224 for colour 2, fill this section with needle weaving checks and stripes no. 1 (*see* page 68), working the warp stitches over the shortest side and using the directional lines to guide you.

129. The weaving in this section will cover the whispy lines of the feathers that encroach from the adjacent feather. This happens throughout the wing. Using the line drawing as your guide, you can draw them back with a washout tailor's pen – or just do them free hand when you get to them. That is up to you.

130. Outline this feather, according to the colour image, with outline stitch using a single strand of 3721.

131. Now work the whispy lines with fly stitch. Use a single strand each of colour variations 4160 and 841 combined and threaded onto the same needle.

132. Starting at the tip of the previous feather, work down the lines, allowing the fly stitch to encroach onto the weaving of that feather.

133. When you reach the lines that encroach on the pink checked feather, come up through the woven checks, working down over the weaving until you are clear of it, then continuing down with all the fly stitch encroaching on the weaving that is on the left.

134. Moving to the feather that is highlighted on the right in the image above, fill it with needle weaving texture no. 3 (*see* page 71).

135. Work the warp stitches across the short side using colour1, Perle #12 842.

136. Work the weft stitches using colour 1, 842 and colour 2, Perle #12 Ecru.

137. When you have completed the weaving, weave a single strand of stranded cotton 840 between rows 1 and 2, following the pattern of row 1.

138. Using the colour image as your guide, work outline stitch around this section using a single strand of 839.

139. Moving to the right, work the highlighted pink feather on the left of the image above with needle weaving texture no. 10 (*see* page 71). Use Perle #12 Ecru for the warp stitches, colour 1.

140. For the weft stitches, use Perle #12 224 for rows 1 to 3 and Perle #12 223 for row 4.

141. Outline this feather with outline stitch using a single strand of 3721.

142. Fill the highlighted beige checked feather with needle weaving checks and stripes no. 1 (*see* page 68) using Perle #12 Ecru for colour 1 and 842 for colour 2.

143. Outline this feather with outline stitch using a single strand of 839.

144. Work the whispy feathers in the same way as described before, using the same threads.

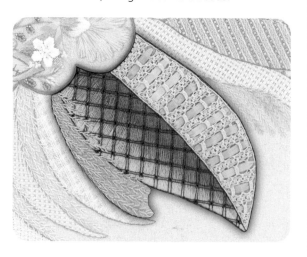

145. Referring to the image below left, start with the far-right section.

146. Following the guidelines for needle-lace filler no. 1 with ribbon inserted (*see* page 66), work backstitch around the entire section using Perle #12 Ecru.

147. Working towards yourself and starting at the base of the feather going to the tip, fill the space with filler no. 1 using the same thread.

148. Use a single strand of stranded cotton 224 to make the twisted cord, threading it through the lace where instructed.

149. Also, where instructed, thread 4 mm ribbon 110 through the needle lace.

150. When you have completed the surrounding embroidery and leaving out the backstitch at the base of the feather, which will be covered later, whip the backstitch that anchors the needle lace with Perle #12 Ecru.

151. Fill the remaining side of this feather with diagonal long and short stitch shading that faces into the vein.

TIP

There are so many ways of doing long and short stitch shading. It is a difficult technique to master and if you have mastered it, my advice is stick to the way that works best for you. I am going to describe how I stitched this section and, other than the colours I used, you are welcome to ignore what I say and do it your own way.

152. Starting adjacent to the vein and using single strands of thread, work with 840 shading through 841 and 842 to 543 at the edge. It may be necessary to do more than a single row of a colour in places to accommodate the size of this section, so that your individual stitches are not too long and unwieldy.

153. Referring to the colour image to guide you and using a single strand of 839, work trellis couching with

cross-stitch filling over the shading. This is found on page 28 and is not to be confused with trellis with cross-stitch couching.

154. Define the sides of this section with outline stitch using 839.

155. Work the whispy feathers in the same way as described before, using the same threads.

156. Fill the woven section highlighted in the image above with needle weaving texture no. 10 (*see* page 72). Use Perle #12 Ecru for the warp stitches, colour 1.

157. For the weft stitches, use Perle #12 224 for rows 1 to 3 and Perle #12 223 for row 4.

158. Outline this feather with outline stitch using a single strand of 3721.

159. Using the colour image to guide you and working with a doubled-over single strand of the same thread, attach a single bead 15° 1883 at regular intervals, adjacent to the outside of the outline stitch, stopping where the whispy feathers will start.

160. With a slight change of thread colours, work the whispy feathers in the same way as described above, using a single strand each of 841 and colour variations 4145 combined and threaded onto the same needle.

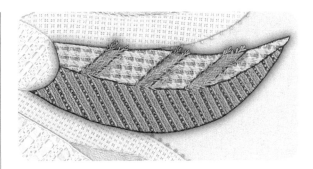

161. Turn your work around so that you are working upside down.

162. Starting with the striped side of the feather, work a line of chain stitch on each line using two strands of 840.

163. With a doubled-over single strand of the same thread, stitch a single bead 15° 650 into each loop created by the chain stitch.

164. Using two strands of 841, work Spanish knotted feather stitch between the chain stitched lines. Leave a small gap between the outer edges of the stitch and the chain stitched line.

165. Using two strands of 543, work fine split stitch in the gaps on either side of the chain stitch/Spanish knotted feather stitch lines.

166. With a doubled-over single strand of 840, stitch a single bead 15° 650 into each loop created by the chain stitch.

167. Moving to the other half of this feather, and using the directional lines to guide you, fill each needle-woven block with needle weaving checks and stripes no. 1 (*see* page 68) using Perle #12 Ecru for colour 1 and Lizbeth #40 693 for colour 2. Work the warp stitches from the outer edge towards the vein.

168. Using a single strand of 838, work outline stitch down the vein between the two halves of the feather, the entire outside edge of both halves and the remaining edges of the needle-woven blocks.

169. Allowing them to encroach upwards into the needle woven blocks and over the vein of the feather, work the whispy feathers in the same way as described previously, using the 841 and colour variations 4145 combination.

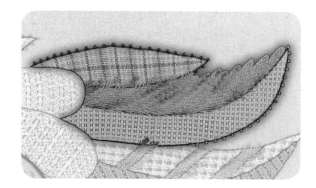

170. Fill the woven section of the light brown feather highlighted in the image above with needle weaving texture no. 10. Use Perle #12 Ecru for the warp stitches, colour 1.

171. For the weft stitches, use Perle #12 842 for rows 1 to 3 and Lizbeth #40 693 for row 4.

172. Outline this half of the feather with outline stitch using a single strand of 839.

173. Using a doubled-over strand of the same thread, attach single beads 15° 650 at regular intervals, adjacent to the outside of the outline stitch on the bottom of the feather, stopping when the line meets the previous feather.

174. Fill the top feather with checks and stripes tartan variation. Work the warp stitches over the shortest side, starting in the middle of the space and working to either side following a colour sequence identical to the rows as listed.

175. Use Perle #12 223 for colour 1, Ecru for colour 2, 842 for colour 3 and 224 for colour 4.

176. Starting in the middle of the space with row 1, work the weft stitches following the colour sequence out to either side.

177. Using the colour image above as your guide, and working with a single strand of 3721, work outline stitch around the bottom and sides of the feathers as needed.

178. Using a doubled-over single strand of the same thread, attach a single bead 15° 1883 at regular intervals, adjacent to the outside of the outline stitch, along the top of the feather, going around the tip and along the bottom line until it meets up with where the whispy feathers start.

179. Allowing them to encroach upwards into the needle woven tartan variation and over the vein of the feather, work the whispy feathers in the same way as described previously, using the 841 and colour variations 4145 combination.

180. Moving inwards to the feathers highlighted in the image above and using perle #12 Ecru, define each of the shapes with backstitch.

181. Working from tip to base, using the backstitch to anchor the needle lace, fill each shape with filler no. 2 (*see* page 66).

182. When the shape becomes too narrow to accommodate the ribbon insertion bars, work only the rows described in points 9, 2 and 3.

183. Towards the base it will become too narrow for even that and you should complete the shape doing rows of single detached buttonhole stitches into each available loop.

184. Use a single strand of stranded cotton 224 to make the twisted cord, threading it through the lace where instructed. Stop when you reach the narrow part where you have done single detached buttonhole stitch rows.

185. Also, where instructed, thread 2 mm ribbon 110 through the needle lace.

186. Whip the backstitch that defines and anchors the needle lace, around each section, with Perle #12 Ecru.

187. Using the image above as your guide, work outline stitch around each shape adjacent to and on the outside of the whipped backstitch using a single strand of 3721. Do not outline the part that abuts the floral centre of the wing.

188. Fill the final wing feather with weaving stitch checks and stripes no. 9 using Perle #12 842 for colour 1 and Ecru for colour 2. Work the warp stitches across the short side.

189. When you have completed the weaving, and working from tip to base, weave a single strand of stranded cotton 840 on each side of the darker stripe that has formed, following the pattern of the darker row on each side.

190. Using the colour image above as your guide, and working with a single strand of 839, work outline stitch around the outside edges of the feather.

191. Using a doubled-over strand of the same thread, attach single beads 15° 650 at regular intervals, adjacent to the outside of the outline stitch.

192. Moving to the floral section inside each wing, fill the petals adjacent to the head with long and short stitch using colour variations 4220, spacing the stitches for multi-coloured thread, as advised in the stitch guide.

193. Work the stem at the base of the petals, and the stems of the stamens with whipped backstitch using two strands of 3051.

194. To spread the colour, take two strands of colour variations 4090, pull them apart and change the direction of the one strand by marrying the end of it with the beginning of the other

195. Using the colour image as your guide, work five two-wrap French knots at the tip of each stamen.

196. Define each blue petal with outline stitch using a single strand of 3746.

197. Moving up, work this flower following the instructions for the golden-brown flower in the owl's tummy.

198. The short stem at the base of the flower is worked with whipped backstitch using two strands of 3051.

199. Using the same thread, place a four-bead lazy-daisy-stitch leaf on each side of the stem.

200. Appearing on the left of the golden-brown flower, the top element is a four-bead flower with three stamens.

201. The bottom element is a six-bead flower with five stamens and a 10-bead leaf.

202. Use the same threads and beads that you have used for all the other flowers, leaves and stamens.

203. Fill the centre of this bloom with long and short stitch using colour variations 4110, spacing the stitches for multi-coloured thread, as advised in the stitch guide.

204. Using a single strand of 3858 stitch, cover a small area of the shading with basic trellis couching, as indicated in the image above.

205. Using two strands of 3859, pad the outside border of this section of the bloom with stem stitch, working up one side and down the other.

206. With a single strand of the same thread, work satin stitch over the padding, starting vertically at the tip and working down each side, fanning the stitch as you go down towards the base.

207. With a single strand of 3858, define the outside with outline stitch.

208. Using the same thread, work outline stitch in the ditch between the outside border and the shaded centre of the bloom.

209. Moving to the green leaves on either side of the bloom, pad each one with horizontal satin stitch using two strands of thread. Work vertical long and short stitch shading over the padding. Use 3053 for the inner leaves and 3052 for the leaves on the outside.

210. Using a single strand of 3051, work fly stitch over the shaded leaves, starting at the tip and working down to the base of each leaf.

211. Using the same thread, define each leaf with outline stitch.

212. Moving to the calyx at the base of the flower, fill each leaf, or petal if you will, with raised herringbone stitch using a single strand of 3858.

213. Using a doubled-over single strand of 4110, pad the little semi-circle at the base of these leaves with horizontal satin stitch.

214. Work a small knot on the back of your work and then snip one side of the thread, thereby changing the thread on your needle to a single strand.

215. Work single strand vertical satin stitch over the padding.

216. Work all the stems highlighted in the image with whipped backstitch using two strands of 3051.

217. Referring back to the instructions for the owl's tummy, work the multiple wrap French-knot buds below and the bullion wrap buds above the bloom in the same way, using the same threads.

218. The lower beaded lazy daisy is worked with eight beads whilst the one closer to the blue buds is a six-bead lazy daisy leaf.

219. Referring to the instructions for the identical flower in the owl's tummy, work this flower in the same way using the same threads.

220. The stems, bullion knot buds and beaded lazy daisy leaves are also worked as you have been doing all along. Some of the beaded lazy daisy leaves are worked with eight beads and the smaller leaves use six beads.

221. The element at the bottom is a six-bead flower with two eight-bead leaves and three stamens, all using the same beads and threads as before.

222. Other than the portion adjacent to the head, outline this floral inner section of the wing with heavy chain stitch using two strands of 3858.

223. Work each scalloped section at the bottom separately as it is impossible to work a continuous line where the curve changes to any great extent.

224. Work a row of outline stitch with a single strand of 3857 on the outside edge of the heavy chain stitch.

This completes one wing. The other wing is a mirror image of this one and should be worked in the same way.

225. Fill the bib below the face of the owl with vertical long and short stitch shading.

226. Turn the project around so that you are working upside down towards the eyes.

227. Starting adjacent to the scallops below the eyes, working from the middle out to each side, returning to the middle to complete the other side and using single strands of thread, work with 840 shading through 841 and 842 to 543 at the edge. It may be necessary to do more than a single row of a colour in places to accommodate the size of this section, so that your individual stitches are not too long and unwieldy.

228. Referring to the colour image to guide you and using a single strand of 839, work trellis couching with cross-stitch filling over the shading. This is found on page 28 and is not to be confused with trellis with cross-stitch couching.

229. When you have completed the beaded fly stitch side feathers described below, define the outside edges of the bib with outline stitch using 839.

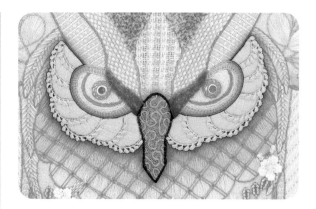

230. Referring to page 59 in the bead embroidery gallery, fill the four feathers on each side of the face with beaded fly stitch. Use a single strand each of 841 and 4160 combined in the same needle and bead 15° 650.

231. Outline each feather individually with outline stitch using a single strand of 839.

232. Moving to the plumage above the eyes, fill the centre feather with needle weaving checks and stripes no. 4 (*see* page 69). Use Perle #12 Ecru for colour 1 and Lizbeth #40 693 for colour 2.

233. Using a single strand of 839, define the feather by working outline stitch around the open edges that do not abut the plumage feathers on either side.

234. Moving to those feathers immediately adjacent to the one you have just done, fill each one with needle weaving checks and stripes no. 13 (*see* page 70) using Perle #12 223 for colour 1, 224 for colour 2 and Ecru for colour 3.

235. Using a single strand of 3721, define the feathers by working outline stitch around the open edges that do not abut the plumage feathers on the outer sides.

236. Moving to the outside feathers of the plumage, fill each one with needle weaving texture no. 10 (*see* page 72). Use Perle #12 Ecru for the warp stitches, colour 1.

237. For the weft stitches, use Lizbeth #40 693 for rows 1 to 3 and Perle #12 842 for row 4.

238. When you have worked the scallops below the eyes, define each of these feathers with outline stitch using a single strand of 839.

239. Following the guidelines for vermicelli couching and the two-thread variation on page 30, fill the beak.

240. Use two strands of 422 couched down with a single strand of the same thread for the first sequence.

241. The second sequence is worked in single strands of 3828.

242. When you have completed the scallops below the eyes, outline the entire beak with whipped back-stitch using two strands of 838.

243. Each scallop is worked in the same way. Using two strands of Ecru, fill the shape with stem stitch padding that runs with the curve of the shape.

244. With a single strand of the same thread, work satin stitch over the padding over the shortest side, i.e. at right angles to the stem stitch padding. It is wise to complete all the padded satin stitch shapes before moving onto the needle-lace borders at the bottom of each one.

245. Starting adjacent to the beak, work around the eye towards the plumage so that, where they meet, each successive needle-lace border lays over the one before it.

246. Using special dentelles #80 and referring to the colour image to guide you, work a line of backstitch around the outside edge of the shape.

247. Referring to the guidelines in the needle-lace techniques gallery and using the same thread, work needle-lace edging no. 9 using the backstitch to anchor each group.

248. Use a single strand of Ecru to anchor the groups, as suggested in the guidelines.

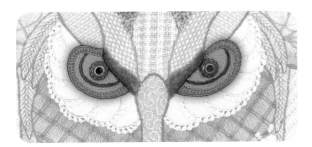

249. Referring to the instructions for caging a flat-back crystal on page 60, attach a crystal 34ss Smoke Topaz over the circle in the middle of the eye with three rows of detached buttonhole stitches.

250. Moving to the outer edge of the eye, work a line of double blanket stitch around the perimeter, starting with the outward facing line which uses two strands of 840.

251. Moving to the inward facing row, use two strands of 842.

252. Using two strands of 839, work heavy chain stitch on the brown line that is within the eyeball.

253. Fill in the remaining space within the eyeball with lines of split stitch using two strands of 543.

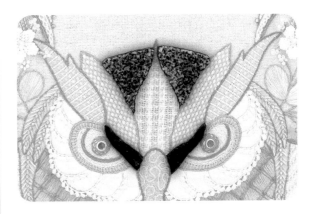

254. Outline the areas on either side of the beak with whipped backstitch using two strands of 838. Using two strands of the same thread and referring page 29, fill the space with tufting (fluffy).

255. Moving to the top of the head, outline the semi-circle that outlines the top of each of the two areas with backstitch using two strands of 839.

256. Combine a single strand each of 4160, 839, 841 and 842 on a size 7 needle. Using this combination of threads, fill the area on each side of the head with fluffy tufting.

Janet

SNAKE

Dimensions: 270 x 215 mm (10⅝ x 8½")

Most people would admit to a primal fear of snakes and I am certainly one of them. They are nevertheless beautiful animals and whilst not a common embroidery subject, are worthy of attention. Let's not forget that they often featured in the Jacobean Tree of Life designs from centuries past. This project constitutes a wide variety of surface stitches.

Materials

FABRIC

450 x 450 mm (17¾ x 17¾") natural coloured cotton linen blend base fabric

450 x 450 mm (17¾ x 17¾") off-white cotton voile backing fabric

EMBROIDERY FRAME

14" embroidery hoop, or
15" x 15" stretcher bars

NEEDLES

Size 7 Embroidery needles
Size 10 Embroidery needles
Size 11 Sharps quilting needles
Size 24 Tapestry needles

THREADS AND BEADS

DMC STRANDED COTTON

ECRU	Ecru
644	Medium Beige Grey
814	Dark Garnet
815	Medium Garnet
816	Garnet
822	Light Beige Grey
3781	Dark Mocha Brown
3865	Winter White

PRECENSIA FINCA PERLE #12

4000	Ultra Very Light Tan

DMC DIAMANT METALLIC THREAD

D140	Black/Antique Gold

MADEIRA METALLIC #40

424	Black/Antique Gold

MIYUKI BEADS

2g	15°	003	Silver Lined Light Gold
2g	15°	592	Antique Ivory Pearl Ceylon

PRECIOSA GLASS PEARLS

3g	2 mm	Cream

PRECIOSA VIVA 12 FLAT-BACK CRYSTALS

2 pieces	20ss Smoke Topaz AB

GENERAL INSTRUCTIONS

- Make sure that the print is taut in the hoop or frame. This will improve the quality of your work.
- Assume that threads are stranded cotton unless otherwise described.
- If you are unsure of any of the stitches, practise on a scrap of fabric before working on the project.
- When working with stranded cotton, use two strands in a size 7 embroidery needle, unless otherwise advised.
- If advised to use a single strand, work with a size 10 embroidery needle.
- Work with a single strand, doubled-over and threaded onto a size 11 sharps quilting or a size 12 bead embroidery needle for all bead embroidery stitches.
- Work with a single strand of Perle, Diamant or Madeira metallic threads.
- Use a size 7 embroidery needle when you work the warp stitches in the weaving.
- Use a size 24 tapestry needle for the weaving weft stitches.

STITCHING INSTRUCTIONS

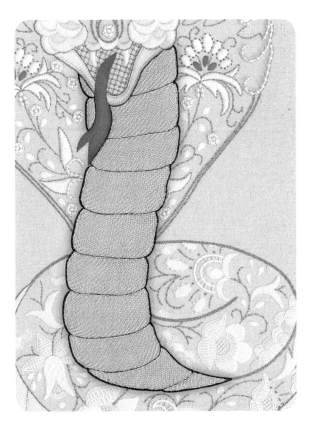

TIP

When needle weaving, I would normally advise that you always go back to the same side to start each weft row so that the pattern is not lost. The woven areas in this project are large and, as a result, you would end up with very long strands of thread at the back of the work. It is for this reason that I have deliberately chosen this weaving pattern, one that makes it easy to go backwards and forwards, using the illustration in the weaving pattern to guide you. The threads used have been calculated using this method.

1. The blocks that constitute the underside of the snake, its belly, are woven and are by far the biggest job in this project. My advice is to start with this – do a few blocks, reward yourself with something else, then keep going back to them in between everything else. In this way, they will not seem tedious.

2. Fill each block with needle weaving texture no. 5 using Finca Perle #12 for both the warp and weft stitches.

3. Surround three sides of each block with Diamant D140 couched down with a single strand of 3781. (The fourth side will be completed by the couching around the previous block.)

4. When you have completed the surrounding embroidery, work a line of outline stitch adjacent to the outside of the metallic thread using a single strand of 3781.

5. In the lower part of the snake, the couched metallic thread forms the outline of the coil. Work this line when you have completed both the weaving and the stitching of the Jacobean elements within the coil.

6. Where the line becomes the outline of the coil, work outline stitch on both sides of the metallic thread couching.

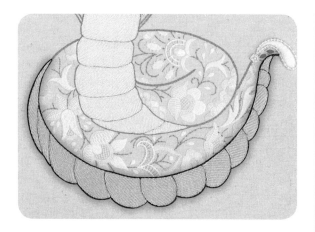

7. Using a single strand of Ecru, work outline stitch adjacent to the inside of the couched metallic thread on all the sides of each block. It should be touching the metallic thread so that it covers the raw edges of the weaving stitches.

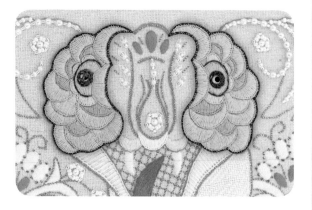

8. Referring to the illustration above right, fill each scale in the face with padded buttonhole stitch. Pad the curved shape with stem stitch using two strands of thread and use a single strand of the same thread, as listed in the table alongside, to work the buttonhole stitch.

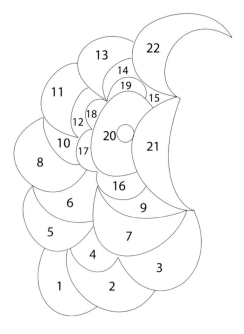

Block	Thread		Block	Thread
1	822		12	644
2	822		13	Ecru
3	822		14	644
4	644		15	644
5	822		16	3865
6	Ecru		17	3865
7	Ecru		18	3865
8	Ecru		19	3865
9	644		20*	Ecru
10	644		21*	Ecru
11	822		22	Ecru

*Before working scales 20 and 21, attach the crystal for the eye as instructed below.

9. Referring to the guidelines for a caged flat-back crystal on page 60, work a 20ss Smoke Topaz AB crystal on the circles provided for the eye using a single strand of 3781.

10. Referring to the colour image to guide you and using a single strand of 3781, work outline stitch on the outside of the buttonhole ridge.

11. The other side of the face is a mirror image of the instructions above.

12. Using a single strand of 3781, couch a line of Diamant D140 around the outside of each section of the face.

13. When you have completed the lower jaw, and working in a continuous line, work outline stitch on the outside of the couched metallic thread.

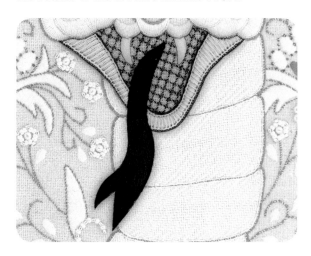

14. Moving to the mouth, fill the inside cavity with basic trellis couching using a single strand of Madeira metallic 424 for the trellis and a single strand of 3781 for the couching.

15. Pad the tongue with stem stitch using two strands of 3782.

16. Work long and short stitch shading over the padding, starting inside the mouth.

17. Use a single strand of 814. Shade through 815 to 816, going back through 815 to 814 at the bottom, forked section of the tongue.

18. When you have completed the surrounding embroidery, define the outside edges of the tongue with outline stitch using a single strand of 814.

19. Pad each half of the lower jaw with stem stitch using two strands of 3782.

20. Work double blanket stitch over the padding using Ecru for the outward facing and 644 for the inward facing rows. In each instance, use two strands of thread.

21. Outline the lower side with Diamant D140 couched down with a single strand of 3781.

22. When you have completed the surrounding embroidery and using a single strand of 3781, work outline stitch adjacent to the outside of the metallic thread line, continuing the outline around the upper part of the head as advised earlier.

23. Using a single strand of 816, work outline stich in the ditch between the double buttonhole stitch and the trellis couching inside the mouth.

24. Pad each of the fangs with stem stitch using two strands of Ecru.

25. Using a single strand of the same thread, work horizontal satin stitch over the padding.

TIP

Padding is usually worked with the same colour thread of the stitch that will be worked over the padding. If, however, the overlying stitch will be worked in varying colours, it is a good idea to work the padding in thread that is as close as possible to the colour of the base fabric.

128

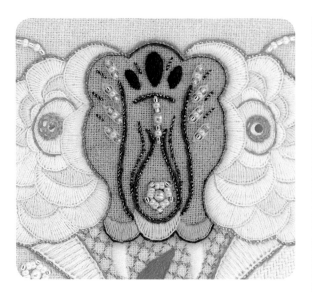

TIP

The bead circle flower features throughout the design and each one is made in the same way using the same threads and beads.

26. Starting at the base of the face, fill each of the scallops with padded buttonhole stitch. Use two strands for the stem stitch padding and a single strand for the buttonhole stitch.

27. Use 3865 for the centre scallop and 644 on the scallops.

28. Using a single strand of 816, define the bottom of these shapes by working a line of outline stitch adjacent to the ridges.

29. Referring to the image above and using a single strand of 3781, couch Diamant D140 on each of the dark lines.

30. Some of these lines are thickened with a row of outline stitch adjacent to the metallic thread worked with a single strand of 3781 as under:

- The curved line that forms the crown of the head – both sides;
- The curved line below the red ovate shapes – both sides;
- The vase shape that defines the inner nose – the outside;
- The two longest lines that define the outer nose – the inside of each line.

31. Referring to the bead circle variation on page 59 and using a doubled-over strand of Ecru thread, create a bead circle flower using a 2 mm cream glass pearl in the centre, 10 beads 15° 592 for the circle and five beads 15° 003 in the final row.

32. Stitch the bead circle flower to the small circle in the centre of the nose.

33. Moving up the nose, using a doubled-over strand of Ecru and starting adjacent to the curved line of metallic thread, bead couch a line of one 15° 003, one 15° 592, one 15° 003, a 2 mm cream glass pearl, one 15° 003, one 15° 592, one 15° 003, going down into the inner nose.

34. Using the same thread, bead couch a line of one 15° 003, one 15° 592 and one 15° 003 on the four lines on each side of the face.

35. Using two strands of 816, pad each of the ovate shapes with horizontal satin stitch.

36. With a single strand of the same thread, work vertical satin stitch over the padding.

37. I am describing the left side of the hood. The right side is a mirror image and should be worked using the same guidelines.

38. Using the same beads and threads described in step 31, work and place a bead circle flower on the dot provided near the top of the head.

39. Each of the bead couching lines that form the outer edge of the hood are worked in the same way – beads 15° 003 alternating with beads 15° 592 or 2 mm cream glass pearls, in varying quantities as listed and stitched on with a doubled-over strand of Ecru thread. Always end with a gold bead. Working from closest to the head, out and around to the side of the hood and always starting at the top **and for each line alternating each bead listed with single beads 15° 003**:

- 1st line – two 15° 592, 10 x 2 mm cream glass pearls, two 15° 592 (start with a gold bead);
- 2nd line – five 15° 592, five 2 mm cream glass pearls, two 15° 592;
- 3rd line – five 15° 592, five 2 mm cream glass pearls, two 15° 592;
- 4th line: Before working the bead line, pad the crescent shape with stem stitch using two strands of Ecru. Using a single strand of the same thread, work horizontal satin stitch over the padding, fanning it as you go around the shape. Thereafter, work the outline, remembering to alternate the listed beads with single beads 15° 003, starting at the top with a gold bead followed by five 15° 592, 16 x 2 mm cream glass pearls and two 15° 592, joining back to the line at the top;
- 5th line – two 15° 592, five 2 mm cream glass pearls, three 15° 592 (start with a gold bead);
- 6th line – three 15° 592, seven 2 mm cream glass pearls, one 15° 592;
- 7th line – two 15° 592, eight 2 mm cream glass pearls, two 15° 592.

40. Using a single strand of 3781 and working close to the bead lines, work outline stitch on the outside of the hood, starting from the head and finishing at the double lines that continue down to the bottom of the hood.

41. Using a single strand of 3781, couch Diamant D140 on the remaining lines that create the leaf shapes in this section of the hood.

42. Moving to the main flower in the hood, pad each of the oval shapes that lie in a semi-circle at the top with vertical satin stitch using two strands of Ecru.

43. Using a single strand of the same thread, work horizontal satin stitch over the padding.

44. When you have completed all the oval shapes and using the colour image to guide you, work single wrap French knots at intervals around each oval shape using Madeira 424.

45. Moving to the lower petals, pad each section of these petals with stem stitch using two strands of Ecru, working along the length of each shape.

46. Working in the opposite direction, over the shortest side of each shape with a single strand of the same thread, cover the padding with satin stitch.

47. Outline each section with Madeira 424 couched down with 3781.

48. Using two strands of 816, pad each of the ovate shapes in the centre of the flower with horizontal satin stitch.

49. With a single strand of the same thread, work vertical satin stitch over the padding.

50. Using a single strand of 3781, couch Diamant D140 on the two lines between the red ovate shapes and on all the tendrils that have been highlighted in the image above.

51. At the tip of the three tendrils closest to the body, place a bead circle flower worked in the same way as those described earlier.

52. Pad the two ovate shapes close to the lower bead circle flower with horizontal satin stitch using two strands of Ecru.

53. With a single strand of the same thread, work vertical satin stitch over the padding.

> **TIP**
>
> Note that these inner tendrils do not appear on the right side of the hood as they have been cut off by the shape of the snake's body.

54. Work the stems below the flower with Diamant D140, couched down with a single strand of 3781.

55. With a doubled-over single strand of Ecru, and referring to the guidelines for attaching single beads on page 58, place five pearls at the tip and on each side of the stem to create the calyx of the large flower.

56. At the end of each side stem, place a bead circle flower worked in the same way as those described earlier.

57. Pad the three ovate shapes close to the stems with horizontal satin stitch using two strands of Ecru.

58. With a single strand of the same thread, work vertical satin stitch over the padding.

59. Moving to the base of the hood, fill the large petals shapes of the flower with vertical rows of stem stitch using two strands of Ecru.

60. Work horizontal satin stitch over the padding.

61. Outline the exposed edges of each petal with Madeira 424 couched into place with a single strand of 3781.

62. Create the tendril coming out of the top of the flower with Diamant D140 couched into place with a single strand of 3781.

63. Bead couch curved lines at the base of each petal. There are two lines and you should start with bead 15° 003, thereafter alternating with bead 15° 592 and ending with a gold bead. Use a doubled-over single strand of Ecru.

64. Worked a bead circle flower as described in step 31 on page 128 and place it on the circle at the base of the hood.

65. Pad the four ovate shapes close to the tendril and close to the bead circle flower, with horizontal satin stitch using two strands of Ecru.

66. With a single strand of the same thread, work vertical satin stitch over the padding.

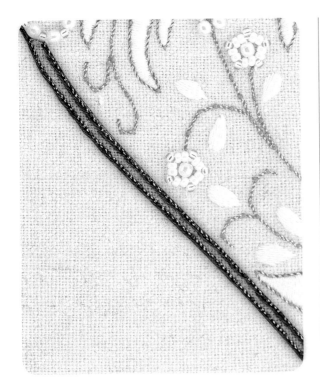

67. Using a single strand of 3781, couch Diamant D140 onto each of the lines that form the border of the lower section of the hood.

68. Still using a single strand of 3781, work outline stitch between the two lines adjacent to and touching the inside line.

69. Work an identical line of outline stitch adjacent to the outside of the outer line.

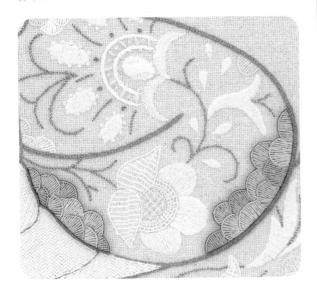

70. Using the image below left to guide you and referring to the illustrations below, fill each semi-circle with buttonhole stitch in a single strand of the stipulated thread.

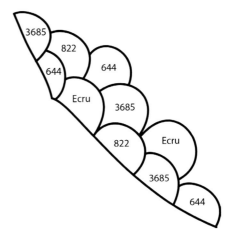

71. Referring to the illustration above, these scales are closest to the underbelly.

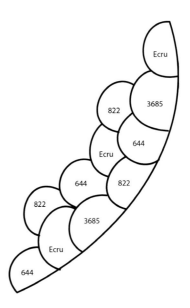

72. Moving along, these scales appear towards the outside, in the same section of the coil.

73. These scales appear throughout the coil and should all be worked in the same way using the threads that are suggested in each illustration.

74. Moving to the flower that lies between the two sections of scales that you have just done, start in the middle of the flower.

75. Fill the centre with variation 2 of trellis with cross-stitch couching found on page 28. Use a single strand of 644.

76. Moving to the outer petals, using 822 for each side petal and Ecru for the one in the centre, outline each petal with split stitch.

77. Thereafter, using a single strand of the relevant colour in each case, work long and short stitch to fill each petal.

78. Using the parallel circular lines to guide you, work layered buttonhole stitch between the centre of the flower and the outer petals. Start at the base with a single strand of 822 followed by a line of Ecru and an outer line worked with 3865.

79. Fill each of the leaves that form the calyx at the base of the flower with long and short stitch using a single strand of 644.

80. Using a single strand of 3865, work loop stitch over the long and short stitch, going from base to tip.

81. With the same thread, work whipped backstitch around each leaf.

82. The flower stem and all its side stems are worked with Diamant D140 couched with a single strand of 3781.

83. Starting in the right-hand top corner, work the buttonhole snake scale with a single strand of 644.

84. Working along the length of the bell-shaped flower, stitch rows of stem stitch padding using two strands of 822.

85. With a single strand of the same thread, work satin stitch over and in the opposite direction to the padding, fanning it around as you go.

86. Pad each small ovate leaf with horizontal satin stitch using two strands of Ecru.

87. With a single strand of the same thread, work vertical satin stitch over the padding.

88. Work the stems and stamens with Diamant D140 couched with a single strand of 3781.

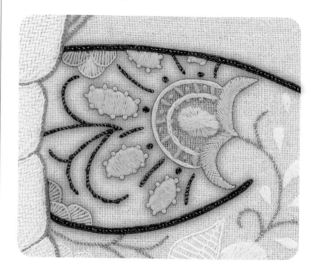

89. Fill the oval shape in the centre of the flower with Rhodes stitch using a single strand of Ecru.

90. Using a single strand of 3865, work heavy chain stitch over each of the semi-circular parallel lines above the oval.

91. Using a single strand of 644, work a short bullion knot on each of the short lines that run between the parallel semi-circles.

92. With the same thread, do a two-wrap French knot between the bullions and below each bullion adjacent to the bottom of the lower line of heavy chain stitch.

93. Outline each calyx leaf at the base with split stitch using 822.

94. With a single strand of the same thread, work each leaf with raised herringbone stitch.

95. Moving to the outer edges of the flower, fill each oval shape with vertical satin stitch padding using two strands of 822.

96. With a single strand of the same thread, work horizontal satin stitch over the padding.

97. Using the colour image to guide you, work evenly spaced two-wrap French knots adjacent to the outer edge of each oval. Use the same thread.

98. Couch Diamant D140 with 3781 on the lines between the ovals and with the same Diamant thread work a two-wrap French knot on each of the dots.

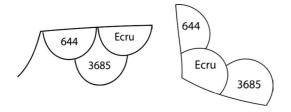

99. Referring to the illustrations above, work the buttonhole snake scales. The image on the left is for the scales at the top whilst the one on the right is for those at bottom left of this section.

100. You are now able to complete the couching that creates the short, inner outline of the snake coil. This is worked with Diamant D140 and 3781. Outline

each side using a single strand of 3781, worked into outline stitch.

101. When it becomes possible, work the outer outline of the coil in the same way.

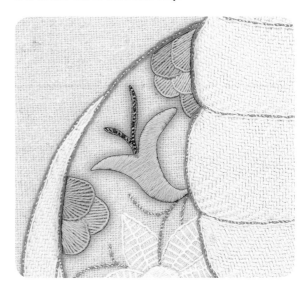

102. Moving to the other side of the underbelly, work the buttonhole circles of the snake scales using the threads described in the illustration below.

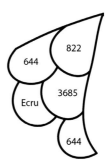

103. Working along the length of the bell-shaped flower, stitch rows of stem stitch padding using two strands of 822.

104. With a single strand of the same thread, work satin stitch over and in the opposite direction to the padding, fanning it around as you go.

105. Work the stems and stamens with Diamant D140 couched with a single strand of 3781.

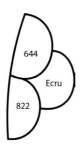

106. Work the buttonhole circles of the snake scales on the left of the colour image using the threads described in the illustration above.

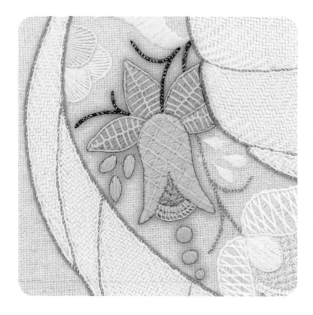

107. Moving anti-clockwise around the coil of the snake, start at the tip of the flower.

108. Fill the centre with variation 2 of trellis with cross-stitch couching found on page 28. Use a single strand of 644.

109. Using the parallel circular lines to guide you, work layered buttonhole stitch to the tip. Start at the base with a single strand of 822, followed by a line of Ecru and an outer line worked with 3865.

110. Moving to the middle of the flower and using Ecru, work a line of split stitch around the bell shape.

111. With a single strand of the same thread, work horizontal satin stitch over the bell shape.

112. Using the same thread, work basic trellis couching over the satin stitch.

113. Fill each of the leaves that form the calyx at the base of the flower with long and short stitch using a single strand of 644.

114. Using a single strand of 3865, work loop stitch over the long and short stitch, going from base to tip.

115. With the same thread, work whipped backstitch around each leaf.

116. Pad the three circles and each small ovate leaf with horizontal satin stitch using two strands of Ecru.

117. With a single strand of the same thread, work vertical satin stitch over the padding.

118. The stems and tendrils are worked with Diamant D140 couched with a single strand of 3781.

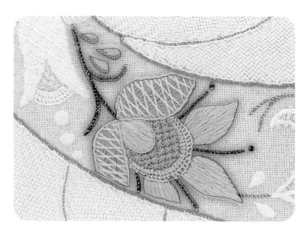

119. Starting in the middle of the flower, fill the centre with variation 2 of trellis with cross-stitch couching (*see* page 28). Use a single strand of 644.

120. Moving to the outer petals, using 822 for each side petal and Ecru for the one in the centre, outline each petal with split stitch.

121. Thereafter, using a single strand of the relevant colour in each case, work long and short stitch to fill each petal.

122. Using the parallel circular lines to guide you, work layered buttonhole stitch between the centre of the flower and the outer petals. Start at the base with a single strand of 822 followed by a line of Ecru and an outer line worked with 3865.

123. Using Ecru, work split stitch around the exposed sides of the oval shape in the very centre of the flower.

124. Using a single strand of the same thread, work

close buttonhole stitch over this shape fanning it slightly into the base.

125. Fill each of the leaves that form the calyx at the base of the flower with long and short stitch using a single strand of 644.

126. Using a single strand of 3865, work back stitch around the leaves.

127. Going from base to tip, work interlaced herringbone stitch over the leaves with the same thread.

128. With the same thread, work whipped backstitch around each leaf.

129. Pad each small ovate leaf with horizontal satin stitch using two strands of Ecru.

130. With a single strand of the same thread, work vertical satin stitch over the padding.

131. The stems and straight tendrils at the top of the flower are worked with Diamant D140 couched with a single strand of 3781.

132. The small dots at the tip of the straight tendril lines are two-wrap French knots worked with D140.

133. Work double blanket stitch on either side of the top of the flower. Use a single strand of 644 for the inward facing and 822 for the outward facing stitches.

134. Using a single strand of 3865, work heavy chain stitch over each of the lines that define the calyx leaves at the base of the flower.

135. Using a single strand of 644, work short bullion knots at intervals within the lines of the calyx leaves.

136. With the same thread, do a two-wrap French knot between the bullions and below each bullion adjacent to the bottom of the lower line of heavy chain stitch.

137. Other than where the two leaves meet and missing the area covered by the double blanket stitch on each side, work a two-wrap French knot above each bullion adjacent to the top of the upper line of heavy chain stitch.

138. Pad the circle in the middle of the flower and, each small ovate leaf with horizontal satin stitch using two strands of Ecru.

139. With a single strand of the same thread, work vertical satin stitch over the padding.

140. The stems and tendrils, including those in the centre of the flower, are worked with Diamant D140 couched with a single strand of 3781.

141. Start in the middle of the flower. Fill the centre with variation 2 of trellis with cross-stitch couching found on page 28. Use a single strand of 644.

142. Using the parallel circular lines to guide you, work layered buttonhole stitch between the centre of the flower and the outer petals. Start at the base with a single strand of 822, followed by a line of Ecru and an outer line worked with 3865.

143. Fill each of the leaves that form the calyx at the base of the flower with long and short stitch using a single strand of 644.

144. Using a single strand of 3865, work loop stitch over the long and short stitch, going from base to tip.

145. With the same thread, work whipped backstitch around each leaf.

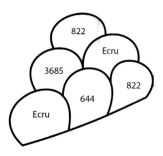

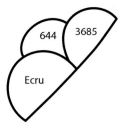

146. Work the buttonhole circles of the snake scales using the threads described in the illustration above.

147. As previously described, each small ovate leaf is padded satin stitch worked with Ecru.

148. The stems and the lines at the top are worked with Diamant D140 couched with a single strand of 3781.

149. The small circles adjacent to the layered buttonhole stitch are two-wrap French knots using D140.

151. Work the buttonhole circles using the threads described in the illustration above.

152. Pad the two leaf shapes above these scales with stem stitch that is worked along the length of each shape. Use two strands of 822 for the one on the left and Ecru for the one on the right.

153. Using a single strand of the same threads, work horizontal satin stitch over the padding.

154. The stems are worked with Diamant D140 couched with a single strand of 3781.

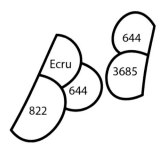

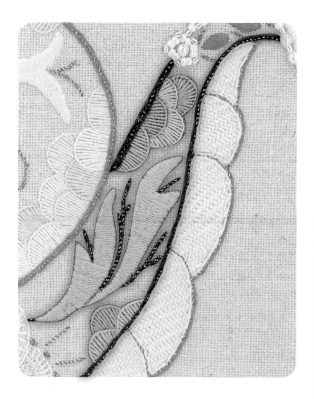

150. Moving towards the end of the coil, start with the snake scales that appear lower down in this image.

155. Work the buttonhole circles towards the top using the threads described in the illustration above.

156. Assuming that you have completed all the weaving in the blocks that constitute the underbelly of the snake, now complete the outline of the coil adjacent to those blocks and, also, the smaller section on the other side.

157. Couch a line of Diamant D140 against the edge of the weaving using a single strand of 3781.

158. Using the same single strand of 3781, outline the edge that faces into the coil of the snake with outline stitch. Don't forget that you need to work Ecru outline stitch all the way around each block on the inside edge.

159. Couch a line of Diamant D140 on the small line on the other side of the coil using a single strand of 3781.

160. Using the same stranded thread, work outline stitch on both sides of and adjacent to the metallic thread.

161. Pad the teardrop curve that forms the tail with stem stitch using two strands of Ecru, running along the length of the curve.

162. With a single strand of Ecru, work satin stitch over the padding. Start at the tip, fanning the stitch around the curve to the narrow base.

163. Using a doubled-over strand of Ecru, bead couch an outline around the satin stitch, working along the top, curving around the shape, going along the bottom and finishing back at the base.

164. Starting with a gold bead 15° 003, alternate with beads 15° 592 until you have added 10 of the cream beads.

165. Still alternating with the gold beads, now add 11 x 2 mm cream glass pearls.

166. Continue to the end alternating beads 15° 003 and 15° 592.

167. Following the previous instructions using the same beads and thread, place a bead circle flower at the base of the bead couched teardrop curve.

168. Using two strands of 816, pad each of the ovate shapes with horizontal satin stitch.

169. With a single strand of the same thread, work vertical satin stitch over the padding.

170. Using a single strand of 3781, couch Diamant D140 on the lines between the red ovate shapes.

Shirley

ELEPHANT

Dimensions: 315 x 255 mm (12³/₈ x 10")

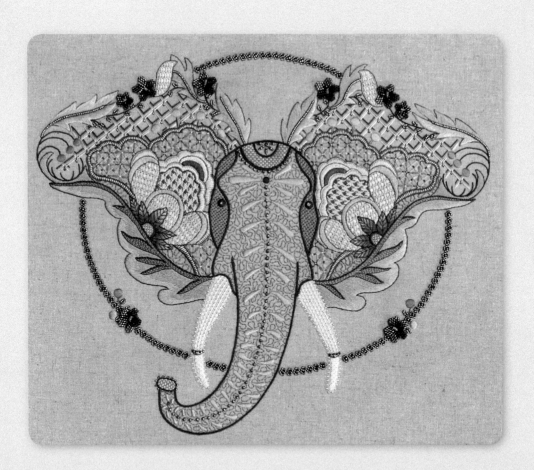

Native to two continents, the African elephant can be identified by its larger
ears which, in this project, have been highlighted with Jacobean elements and
three-dimensional beadwork flowers. The design is finished off with a circle
of daisy chain, a traditional Zulu beadwork technique.

Materials

FABRIC

550 x 450 mm (21½ x 18") natural coloured cotton
   linen blend base fabric
550 x 450 mm (21½ x 18") off-white cotton voile
   backing fabric

EMBROIDERY FRAME

18" x 14" stretcher bars

NEEDLES

Size 7 Embroidery needles
Size 10 Embroidery needles
Size 11 Sharps quilting needles
Size 12 Long beading needles
Size 26 Tapestry needles

THREADS AND BEADS

DMC STRANDED COTTON

ECRU	Ecru
315	Medium Dark Antique Mauve
316	Medium Antique Mauve
520	Dark Fern Green
522	Fern Green
523	Light Fern Green
524	Very Light Fern Green
646	Dark Beaver Grey x 2
648	Light Beaver Grey
778	Very Light Antique Mauve
844	Ultra Dark Beaver Grey x 2
3072	Very Light Beaver Grey
3726	Dark Antique Mauve
3782	Light Mocha Brown

DMC DENTELLES #80

ECRU   Ecru x 2

DMC PERLE #12

524	Very Light Fern Green
778	Very Light Antique Mauve

PRESENCIA FINCA PERLE #12

4000	Ultra Very Light Tan
1984	Dark Antique Mauve

SUPERLON BEADING THREAD AA

Burgundy
Grey

DI VAN NIEKERK HAND-PAINTED SILK RIBBON

2 mm No. 134 Ecru

MIYUKI BEADS

Size 15°

4g	15° 650	Rustic Grey SL Alabaster
2g	15° 1630	Semi-Matte SL Moss Green
2g	15° 2442	Crystal Ivory Gold Luster

Size 11°

2g	11° 4557	Vitrail Matte
4g	11° 4571	Magic Orchid

Size 8°

2g	8° 4557	Vitrail Matte

Size 11° Delica Beads

6g	DB11-108	Cinnamon Gold Luster

PRECIOSA VIVA 12 FLAT-BACK CRYSTALS

2 pieces   20ss Smoke Topaz AB

GENERAL INSTRUCTIONS

- Stretch the fabric print over 18" x 14" stretcher bars. The original was worked on Edmunds stretcher bars.
- Make sure that the print is taut. This will improve the quality of your work.
- Assume that threads are stranded cotton unless otherwise described.
- If you are unsure of any of the stitches, practise on a scrap of fabric before working on the project.
- When working with stranded cotton, use two strands in a size 7 embroidery needle, unless otherwise advised.
- If advised to use a single strand, work with a size 10 embroidery needle.
- Work with a single strand, doubled over and threaded onto a size 11 sharps quilting needle for all bead embroidery stitches.
- Work with a long beading needle and beading thread when constructing the three-dimensional beaded elements.
- Work with a single strand of Perle and Dentelles threads.
- Use a size 7 embroidery needle when you work the warp stitches in the weaving.
- Use a size 26 tapestry needle for the weaving's weft stitches and the needle-lace detached buttonhole stitches.

STITCHING INSTRUCTIONS

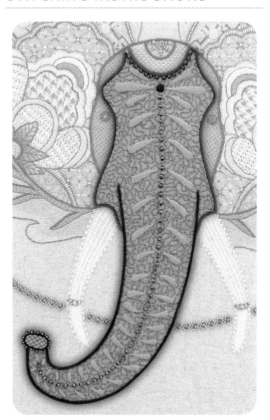

1. Work the main area of the trunk with Vermicelli couching using two strands of 646 couched down with a single strand of the same colour. To ensure unbroken curves in the couching, work over the entire area, ignoring the lines of the curved teardrop and other shapes that go down the trunk. You will work these shapes later by going over the couching.

2. Pad the circle at the top of the trunk, just above where the bead line starts, with horizontal satin stitch using two strands of 844.

3. With a single strand of the same thread, work vertical satin stitch over the padding.

4. The curved teardrop shapes on either side of the centre line are worked in the same way with the shapes on the one side being a mirror image of those on the other.

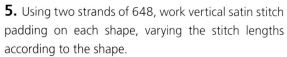

5. Using two strands of 648, work vertical satin stitch padding on each shape, varying the stitch lengths according to the shape.

6. With a single strand of the same thread, work diagonal satin stitch over the padding.

7. Using a doubled-over strand of 646, attach single beads 11° 4557 to each of the small dots that run down the centre of the trunk.

8. Outline each side of the trunk with heavy chain stitch using two strands of 844.

9. Referring to the instructions for basic double weaving on page 68, fill the oval shape that forms the trumpet at the end of the trunk. Use two strands of 646 for the warp and two strands of 648 for the weft stitches.

10. Using 844, work backstitch around the weaving with two strands, whipping the backstitch with a single strand of the same colour.

11. Using a doubled-over strand of 646, attach single beads 15° 650 at intervals around the trumpet.

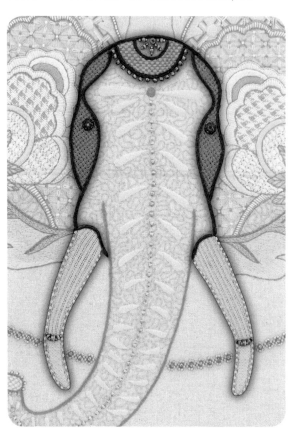

12. Referring to variation 2 of trellis with cross-stitch couching on page 28 and using a single strand of 844, fill the two sides of the face leaving a gap for the eye, as indicated by the small circle, on each side.

13. Following the guidelines for the caged flat-back crystal on page 60, attach a smoke topaz AB crystal over the circle provided for each eye using a single strand of 844. Take note that for a size 20ss crystal you will require only two rows of detached button-hole stitch.

14. Moving to the top of the head, fill the semi-circle between the two lines with double weaving. Use two strands of 646 for the warp and two strands of 648 for the weft stitches.

15. Using two strands of 844, outline the top and bottom edges with heavy chain stitch.

16. Using a doubled-over strand of 646, attach single beads 11° 4557 at intervals on the outside of the bottom edge.

17. Referring to page 58 and using the guidelines for attaching a bead with a bead, place a bead 8° 4557 held down with a 15° 650 stopper bead on the small circle within in the small circle at the top of the head. Use a doubled-over strand of 646.

18. On each of the radiating lines in that semi-circle couch a small line of beads 15° 650, 11° 4557 and 15° 650 using the same thread.

19. Moving to the tusks, pad the lower portion with vertical stem stitch lines using two strands of Ecru.

20. With a single strand of the same thread, work horizontal satin stitch over the padding.

21. With the same thread, work diagonal basic trellis couching over the satin stitch.

22. Referring to the pattern for texture no. 2 on page 71, fill the upper part of the tusk using perle #12 4000. Place the warp stitches horizontally over the shortest side with the weft stitches being worked along the length of the tusk.

23. Bead couch a line of beads 15° 650, 11° 4557, 15° 650, 8° 4557, 15° 650, 11° 4557 and 15° 650 in the break between the two sections of the tusk. Allow them to lie in a natural curve and couch them down where they sit.

24. When you have completed any surrounding embroidery, define each section of the tusk with outline stitch using a single strand of Ecru.

25. With a doubled-over strand of the same thread, place single beads 15° 2442 at regular intervals on the outside of the outline all the way around each tusk.

26. When you have completed all adjacent embroidery, and using two strands of 844, work heavy chain stitch on all the remaining outlines of the face.

Moving to the elephant's ears, each one is worked in the same way. The right ear is described and the left ear is a mirror image of that one.

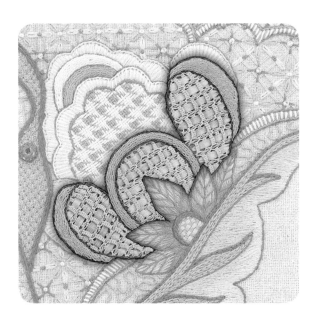

27. Following the guidelines for filler no. 3 on page 67 and using Dentelles #80 Ecru, work backstitch around the outer circular edge of the middle of each of these petals. The size of the backstitch would aim to accommodate two detached buttonhole stitches, with a bit of wiggle room.

28. Work the needle-lace filler using the same thread.

29. Following the instructions for ribbon and twisted thread insertion on page 67, use a single strand of 778 for the twisted thread and 2 mm Di van Niekerk hand-painted ribbon no. 134.

30. The green outer borders of each of these petals is worked with DMC Perle #12 524 following the guidelines for raised stem stitch on page 26. Work the stitch ladder between the parallel lines that form the border, making them fan as you go around the circle.

31. When you have completed the embroidery adjacent to the outside of these petals, work outline stitch around the outer edges of each petal and in the ditch between the needle-lace centre and the raised stem stitch border. Use a single strand of 520.

32. Fill the centre of the flower with needle weaving checks and stripes no. 1 on page 68, using Finca Perle #12. Use 4000 for colour 1 and 1984 for colour 2.

33. When you have completed the padded striped blanket stitch that surrounds this section, define the edge of the weaving with outline stitch using a single strand of 315.

34. Moving to the two crescent shapes above the padded striped blanket stitch, fill the lower shape with raised stem stitch using Finca Perle #12 1984.

35. Fill the top shape with raised stem stitch using Finca Perle #12 4000.

36. When you have completed the padded striped blanket stitch surrounding these shapes, define each one with outline stitch using a single strand of 315.

37. Moving to the bottom of the flower, pad each petal separately with horizontal satin stitch using two strands of 3782.

38. Fill each petal with long and short stitch shading. Using single threads, start with 3726 at the base, shading through 316 to 778 at the tip.

39. Using a single strand of 315, work wide fly stitch, from tip to base, over the shading.

40. Using 646, work vermicelli couching in the spaces on either side of this flower. Thereafter, outline each petal using a single strand of 315.

41. Fill the semi-circle at the base of the petals with double weaving. Use two strands of 646 for the warp and two strands of 648 for the weft stitches.

42. Using two strands of 844, outline the semi-circle, not including the bottom, with heavy chain stitch.

43. The basis of the embellishment in these outer petals is trellis couching with cross-stitch filling which is found on page 28.

44. Work the long stitches on the double lines with two strands of 522.

45. The four stitches of the cross at the intersections of the double lines should be worked with two strands of 520. As you move between the crosses, work a two-wrap French knot in the middle of the double lines, between the intersections at the point where the two ovate leaf shapes meet.

46. Using two strands of 524, work a detached chain stitch on each of those ovate shapes.

47. Using two strands of 316, work a detached chain stitch on each of the ovate shapes that are in the large block.

48. Using a single, doubled-over strand of Ecru on a bead embroidery needle-stitch a single bead 15° 2442 in the centre of the pink 'flower' and in the centre of the green crosses where the four stitches meet.

49. Using two strands of Ecru, pad the outside border of each section that forms the border of each section of these outer petals. Fill the space between the double lines with stem stitch.

50. Using two strands of 3726 and following the guidelines for striped blanket stitch in the embroidery

stitches gallery, work the blanket stitch with the ridge facing outwards.

51. Work the straight stitches that create the second stripe with two strands of Ecru.

52. Using a single strand of 315, work outline stitch at the base of the striped blanket stitch.

53. When you have completed the surrounding embroidery and using the same thread, work outline stitch adjacent to and touching the ridge at the top of the blanket stitch.

54. Return to the inside of the flower to complete the remaining borders that surround the elements of the flower. Each one is filled with padded striped blanket stitch and you will want to make sure that the ridge that forms lays over any raw edges that have been created when stitching neighbouring sections.

55. Pad each area with stem stitch using two strands of 3782.

56. Starting at the top, the pink section uses two strands of 778 for the blanket stitch and Ecru for the straight stitch. Work outline stitch adjacent to the outside of the ridge using a single strand of 315.

57. The green section adjacent to the woven centre uses two strands of Ecru for the blanket stitch and 524 for the straight stitch. Work outline stitch adjacent to the outside of the ridge using a single strand of 520.

58. The remaining pink sections lower down and on each side, are worked in the same way using the same threads as the pink section at the top.

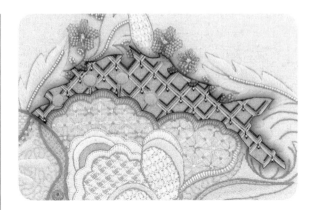

59. Leaving gaps where necessary for the pink circles and their stems, work battlement couching on the lines provided.

60. Using the image above as your guide, start on the lines with two strands of 844.

> **TIP**
>
> Battlement couching creates a woven effect where the lines intersect. It is important that you complete all the stitches systematically, completing the first layer followed by the second layer that goes at right angles to the first, before moving onto the next colour and complete each colour similarly systematically. If you don't do it this way, the weave won't happen.

61. Working downwards and inwards, complete the battlement couching using two strands of 646 followed by 648 and finally 3072.

62. Work the couching stitch over the intersection of the 3072 stitches using a doubled-over strand of 844 on a bead embroidery needle. Work the stitch and immediately attach a single bead 15° 650 below it.

63. Moving to the pink circles, pad each one with horizontal satin stitch using two strands of 778.

64. Work vertical satin stitch over the padding using a single strand of 778.

65. The stem leading up to each of the circles is a bullion knot worked with two strands of 522.

146

66. With a single strand of 520, work a few outline stitches up one side of the bullion knot.

67. Fill the major part of this leaf shape, forming the bottom of the ear with long and short stitch shading.

TIP

There are so many ways of doing long and short stitch shading. It is a difficult technique to master and if you have mastered it, my advice is stick to the way that works best for you. I describe below how I stitched this section and other than the colours I used, you are welcome to ignore what I say and do it your own way.

68. Working from the inside closest to the vein and using a single strand of thread, start with 522, shading through 523 to 524.

69. Using the colour image as your guide, shade out to 778 where you need the pink to appear.

70. Using two strands of 844, work a line of chain stitch up the main vein on the side closest to the Jacobean flower.

71. With the same thread, work single lines of chain stitch on the top edge of each of the side veins.

72. Using two strands of 646, fill the remaining areas of both the side and main veins with lines of chain stitch. Stitch longer and shorter rows as necessary.

73. With a single strand of 844, work outline stitch around the outer edge of the veins.

74. With the same thread, define the edge of the long and short stitch shading leaf with outline stitch.

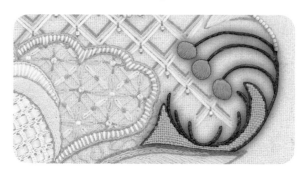

75. Moving around the outside of the ear, fill the pink semi-crescent shape with single weaving using Perle #12 778.

76. With two strands of 844, work whipped backstitch on the curved lines, arising from the woven area.

77. Using the same thread work the stems for the pink circles in whipped backstitch, starting at the base adjacent to the side of the woven area and continuing up to the circles.

78. You will be left with a small area on each side of the crescent that has not been outlined. Define these areas in outline stitch using a single strand of 315.

79. Using two strands of 316, pad each of the circles with horizontal satin stitch.

80. With a single strand of the same thread, work vertical satin stitch over the padding.

81. Using two strands of 3782, pack each side of the leaf with stem stitch which runs along the length of the leaf parallel to the vein.

82. Work diagonal long and short stitch over the padding, starting adjacent to the vein on both sides using a single strand of 522.

83. On the top side shade through 524 to 778, using the image above as your guide.

84. On the bottom side, shade through to 524 on the edge.

85. Using a doubled-over strand of 520, bead couch beads 15° 1630 along the stem and up the vein.

86. With a single strand of 520 and using the image above as your guide, work intermittent lines of outline stitch to define the edges of the leaf.

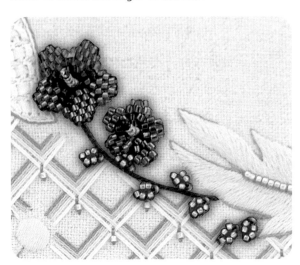

87. Work the stem of this branch of flowers and the smaller stem that comes out of the large leaf, with whipped backstitch using two strands of 844.

88. With a doubled-over strand of 520 on a bead embroidery needle, and referring to page 59, place beaded lazy daisy leaves where necessary. Each leaf is worked using 6 beads 15° 1630.

89. Referring again to the bead embroidery gallery and using bead DB11-108 with the burgundy beading thread on the bead embroidery needle make a six-bead flower (*see* page 37) and a four-bead flower (*see* page 35).

TIP

Because your thread would be inclined to snag while stitching, you might like to consider making the three-dimensional beaded elements, but only attaching them to the fabric later.

90. Following the guidelines on page 34 for attaching three-dimensional elements to fabric, attach the larger flower to the tip of the stem, with the smaller flower being attached below that. Use the tails of thread already on the flower but do not end off.

91. Using the same thread, make a small stamen in the centre of each flower. Come up in the gap where the petals meet, pick up four beads 15° 2442 for the six-bead flower, three beads for the four-bead flower and one bead 4571. Return down the cream beads and go back into the fabric, ending off the threads.

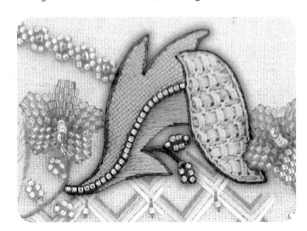

92. Following the guidelines for filler no. 3 on page 67 and using Dentelles #80 Ecru, work backstitch around the outer edge of the leaf shape on the right. The size of the backstitch would aim to accommodate two detached buttonhole stitches, with a bit of wiggle room.

93. Work the needle-lace filler using the same thread.

94. Following the instructions for ribbon and twisted thread insertion, use a single strand of 778 for the twisted thread and 2 mm Di van Niekerk hand-painted ribbon no. 134.

95. Using Dentelles #80 Ecru, whip the backstitch that defines the needle-lace shape.

96. When you have completed the surrounding embroidery and using a single strand of 844, work outline stitch around the shape adjacent to the outside of the whipped backstitch.

97. Fill the top section of the leaf on the right with single weaving using Perle # 12 524.

98. Using two strands of 3782, pad the lower half of the leaf with lines of stem stitch that run parallel to the vein.

99. Work diagonal long and short stitch shading over the padding starting adjacent to the vein with a single strand of 522 shading out to 524.

100. Work the small leaf stem that comes out of the bottom half of the leaf with whipped backstitch using two strands of 844.

101. With a doubled-over strand of 520 on a bead embroidery needle, and referring to page 59, place two beaded lazy daisy leaves where necessary. Each leaf is worked using six beads 15° 1630.

102. Using a doubled-over strand of 520, bead couch beads 15° 1630 up the vein.

103. With a single strand of 520 and using the image above as your guide, work intermittent lines of outline stitch to define the edges of the lower half of the leaf.

104. With the same thread, work outline stitch all the way around the weaving that forms the upper half of the leaf.

105. Using two strands of 3782, pack each side of the leaf with stem stitch which runs along the length of the leaf parallel to the vein.

106. Work diagonal long and short stitch over the padding, starting adjacent to the vein on both sides using a single strand of 522.

107. On the left side, shade through 524 to 778, using the image above as your guide.

108. On the right side, shade through to 524 on the edge.

109. Using a doubled-over strand of 520 bead couch beads 15° 1630 up the vein.

110. With a single strand of 520 and using the image above as your guide, work intermittent lines of outline stitch to define the edges of the leaf.

111. Work the stem of the flower branch with whipped backstitch using two strands of 844.

112. With a doubled-over strand of 520 on a bead embroidery needle, and referring to page 59, place beaded lazy daisy leaves where necessary. Each leaf is worked using six beads 15° 1630.

113. Referring again to the bead embroidery gallery and using bead DB11-108 with the burgundy beading thread on the bead embroidery needle make a six-bead flower (*see* page 37).

114. Following the guidelines for attaching three-dimensional elements to the fabric, attach the larger flower to the tip of the stem and using the same thread, make a small stamen in the centre of the flower using four beads 15° 2442 and one bead 4571. Return down the cream beads and go back into the fabric, ending off the threads.

The left ear is worked in the same way, creating a mirror image of the right ear described above.

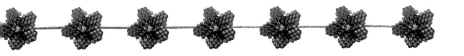

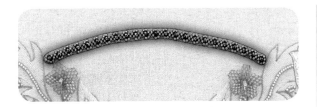

115. Moving to the oval border line between the ears and following the instructions for the linked daisy chain braid (*see* page 61) work a daisy chain that comprises 23 circles. You need to bear in mind that everyone's beading tension is slightly different and you might require fewer circles. It should be either the same length as the line, or slightly shorter so that you will stretch it slightly to fit.

116. Work with grey beading thread on the bead embroidery needle using bead 11° 4571 encircled with eight 15° 650 beads.

117. Stitch it to the fabric using the tails of beading thread, attaching it on each end then working towards the centre from both sides, stretching it evenly over the space.

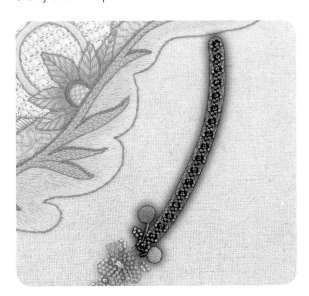

118. Moving to the border lines below the elephant, start by working the small circle flowers.

119. The stem leading up to each of the circles is a couched bullion knot worked with two strands of 522. Couch it into a curved shape with one or two stitches worked with a single strand of the same thread.

120. With a single strand of 520, work a few outline stitches up one side of the curved bullion knot.

121. Work the inward facing circle with 316 and the outward facing circle with 778.

122. Pad the circle with horizontal satin stitch using two strands of thread. Work vertical satin stitch over the padding with a single strand.

123. Coming off the stems are six-bead beaded lazy daisies. Work these after you have attached the daisy chain using thread 520 and beads 15° 1630.

124. For the right side of the design, work 20 circles of daisy chain braid, using the same beads and threads that you used for the braid between the ears. The left side requires 19 bead circles.

125. When you attach the braid, stop slightly before that small circle provided for the three-dimensional flower.

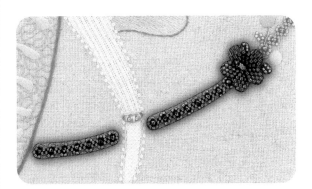

126. On the right side of the project the daisy chain braid between the three-dimensional flower and the tusk requires eight circles. Between the tusk and the trunk, you will require seven circles.

127. On the left side of the project work 10 circles between the flower and the tusk. Work three circles between the tusk and the trunk.

128. On each side, you will need to stitch and place a six-bead flower using beads DB11-108 and burgundy thread. The stamen in the middle of the flower is worked with four beads 15° 2442 and a bead 11° 4571 at the tip.

129. Using the image above as your guide, work two six-bead beaded lazy daisy stitches to create leaves radiating out from the beaded flower.

Roger

RHINO

Dimensions: 430 x 315 mm (17 x 12³/₈")

This huge and interesting animal, a throwback to the time of the dinosaurs, is critically endangered because of poaching. Whilst rhinos are normally seen with tick birds perching on their backs, Roger has been prettied up with Jacobean flowers instead. Don't be frightened by the plethora of stitches that create the texture of the animal's hide as well as the tree, trunk and leaf umbrella. It's easy once you get started.

151

Materials

FABRIC

550 x 450 mm (21½ x 18") natural coloured cotton linen blend base fabric

550 x 450 mm (21½ x 18") off-white cotton voile backing fabric

EMBROIDERY FRAME

22" x 16" stretcher bars

NEEDLES

Size 7 Embroidery needles
Size 10 Embroidery needles
Size 11 Sharps quilting needles
Size 12 Long beading needles
Size 26 Tapestry needles

THREADS AND BEADS

DMC STRANDED COTTON

ECRU	Ecru
150	Ultra Very Dark Dusty Rose
151	Very Light Dusty Rose
611	Drab Brown
613	Very Light Drab Brown
646	Dark Beaver Grey
648	Light Beaver Grey x 2
772	Very Light Yellow Green
844	Ultra Dark Beaver Grey
924	Very Dark Grey Blue
926	Medium Grey Blue
927	Light Grey Blue
951	Light Tawny
3345	Dark Hunter Green
3346	Hunter Green
3347	Medium Yellow Green
3348	Light Yellow Green
3350	Ultra Dark Dusty Rose
3354	Light Dusty Rose
3731	Very Dark Dusty Rose
3733	Dusty Rose
3768	Dark Grey Blue
3835	Medium Grape
3836	Light Grape
3856	Ultra Very Light Mahogany

CHAMELEON STRANDED COTTON

66	Rustic Brick
127	Woodland x 2

PRESENCIA FINCA PERLE #12

3000	Ecru
4799	Ultra Very Light Moss Green

DMC PERLE #12

927	Light Grey Blue

SUPERLON BEADING THREAD AA

Dusty Rose
Light Orchid
Olive
Cream

MIYUKI BEADS
Size 15°

4g	15°	356	Purple Line Amethyst AB
4g	15°	459	Metallic Olive
4g	15°	553	Dark Peach SL Alabaster
2g	15°	574	Lilac SL Alabaster
2g	15°	642	Salmon SL Alabaster
2g	15°	650	SL Rustic Grey Alabaster
2g	15°	1631	Semi-Matte SL Saffron
4g	15°	2210	Grey Lined Crystal AB

Size 11°

2g	11°	577	Butter Cream Gold Lined Alabaster
4g	11°	4557	Vitrail Matte

Size 8°

4g	8°	4557	Vitrail Matte
2g	8°	2035	Matte Metallic Khaki Iris

PRECIOSA VIVA 12 FLAT-BACK CRYSTALS

1 piece   20ss Smoke Topaz AB

GENERAL INSTRUCTIONS

- Stretch the fabric print over 22" x 16" stretcher bars. The original was worked on Edmunds stretcher bars.
- Make sure that the print is taut. This will improve the quality of your work.
- Assume that threads are stranded cotton unless otherwise described.
- If you are unsure of any of the stitches, practise on a scrap of fabric before working on the project.
- When working with stranded cotton, use two strands in a size 7 embroidery needle, unless otherwise advised.
- If advised to use a single strand, work with a size 10 embroidery needle.
- Work with a single strand, doubled over and threaded onto a size 11 sharps quilting needle for all bead embroidery stitches.
- Work with a long beading needle and beading thread when constructing the three-dimensional beaded elements.
- Work with a single strand of Perle thread.
- Use a size 7 embroidery needle when you work the warp stitches in the weaving.
- Use a size 26 tapestry needle for the weaving weft stitches.

FREESTYLE STITCHING INDEX

The hide of the rhinoceros along with the trunk and leaf areas of the tree are filled with freestyle stitching using a variety of stitches. It is important to note that the shape of the areas filled with specific stitches should be irregular, no squares or circles, and that other than at the edges, the areas filled should not line up with any other areas that have been filled with different stitches. Intersperse your stitching with single-wrap French knots to soften the effect and, also, to fill up spaces that can't be filled with the recommended stitches. You are aiming to create an overall texture.

The index alongside provides a numbered diagram for each stitch sequence used, along with a brief description of what each diagram means. The numbers correlate with the colour images in the stitching instructions where the threads you should use are listed.

Code	Diagram	Description
1		Single weaving shading variation: see needle weaving techniques gallery, page 68
2		Trellis couching – cross stitch filling: see embroidery stitches gallery, page 28
3		Trellis couching – basic (diagonal): see embroidery stitches gallery, page 27
4		Buttonhole circle/half/semi-circle: see embroidery stitches gallery, page 19
5		5-petal buttonhole flower/half flower (with 3 to 5 French knots in the centre): see embroidery stitches gallery, page 22
6		9-petal lazy daisy stitch flower/half flower with French knot centre with or without couched stem: see embroidery stitches gallery, pages 18-31
7		3 lazy daisy petals, French knot at bottom, couched stem with lazy daisy leaves: see embroidery stitches gallery, pages 18-31

Code	Diagram	Description
8		Sheaf stitch: see embroidery stitches gallery, page 26
9		Fly stitch: see embroidery stitches gallery, page 22
10		Feather stitch: see embroidery stitches gallery, page 22
11		Loose French knot: see embroidery stitches gallery, page 23
12		Couched stem, buttonhole semi-circle petals, 3 to 5 French knots at tip, lazy daisy leaves: all stitches see embroidery stitch gallery, pages 18-31
13		Cretan stitch leaf: see embroidery stitches gallery, page 21

STITCHING INSTRUCTIONS

1. Using two strands of 844, work a whipped back-stitch outline around each of the horns. Referring to the image above, also work the two wrinkles that come down between the two horns.

2. With a doubled-over single strand of 648, following the guidelines for attaching a bead with a bead on page 58, fill the front larger horn with beads 8° 4557 held down with beads 15° 2210. Start at the tip of the horn with a single bead, followed by curved rows that get longer as the horn widens to the base. Stitch the beads down as close as possible.

3. Working in the same way with the same threads, fill the smaller horn with beads 11° 4557 held down with beads 15° 2210.

4. Referring to the guidelines for caging a 20ss flat-back crystal in the bead embroidery gallery, use a single strand of 844 to attach the crystal over the small circle that depicts the pupil of the eye.

5. Fill the eyeball area up to the line partly surrounding the pupil with semi-circles of split stitch using two strands of Ecru.

6. Define the outer edge of the eyeball with outline stitch using a single strand of 844.

7. Referring to the instructions for shading with single

weaving in the needle weaving gallery and using the colour image as your guide, partially fill the rest of the eye using a single strand of 844.

8. Using two strands of the same colour, outline the eye with whipped backstitch.

9. Now working with a single strand of the same thread, 844, couch eyelashes on the lines provided.

10. The wrinkles above and below the eye are whipped backstitch. Use two strands of 844 to work the backstitch and a single strand of the same thread to whip. For the purposes of these instructions I am going to call this 2:1 whipped backstitch.

11. Moving to the nose, partially fill the nostril with shading with single weaving using a single strand of 844.

12. Fill the solid area that depicts the mouth, below the nose, with split stitch using two strands of 844.

13. Work 2:1 whipped backstitch using 844 on all the lines of the nose and mouth, outlining the nostril at the same time.

14. Refer to the freestyle stitching index to identify the numbered stitches in the colour image below left.

15. Use a single strand of 646 for the darker areas at the bottom and right side of the face, slowly moving to a single strand of 648 for the lighter, inner parts of the face. This requires that you work stitches in one or other of the threads in the same area as the two shades merge.

16. All outlines around the edge of the face are 2:1 whipped backstitch worked with 844.

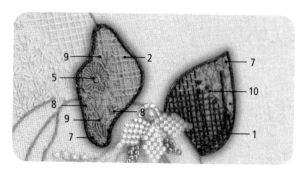

17. The ears are worked referring to the freestyle stitching index.

18. Starting on the left of the left ear, use 646 merging into 648 on the right side of the ear.

19. Starting at the bottom of the right ear, use 844 merging into 646 at the top of the ear.

20. Work the line that runs down within the right ear, as well as the outline of both ears with 2:1 whipped backstitch using 844.

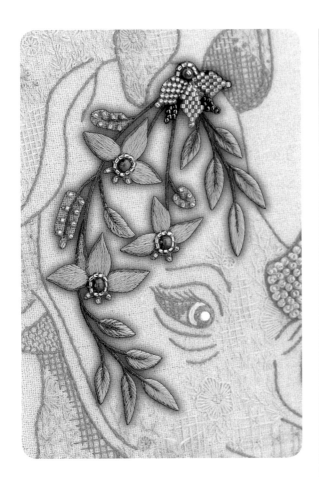

21. All the small leaves are filled with diagonal long and short stitch shading which faces into the vein of the leaf.

22. Each leaf is blue against the vein shading out to green on the edge as under:

- The single leaves at the tip of each stem use a single strand each of 927 and 772;
- The pair below the tip uses a single strand each of 926 and 3348;
- The pair at the base of each stem uses a single strand each of 3768 and 3348;
- The single leaf between the orchids uses a single strand each of 926 and 3348.

23. With a single strand of 3768, define the left side of each leaf with outline stitch worked from base to tip.

24. Working from base to tip, work stem stitch along each stem using two strands of 924, continuing up the vein of the leaf. Bring the needle up from under the stem stitch at the base of the leaf and whip the

stem stitch back down to the bottom (this does not include the vein of the leaf).

25. Using two strands of 648, pad each petal of the 3-petal orchid with horizontal satin stitch.

26. Work single strand vertical long and short stitch shading over the padding using 3856 at the base of each petal shading up to 3354 at the tip.

27. Work the stem of each flower and the bead bud stems in whipped stem stitch using two strands of 3731.

28. Using the colour image alongside to guide you, define one side of each petal with outline stitch using a single strand of 3731.

29. Using a doubled-over single strand of 648 and following the guidelines for attaching a single bead on page 58, attach a bead 8° 2035 in middle of each flower.

30. Bring the needle up next to that bead and following the instructions for bead circles on page 58, work a circle of 10 beads 15° 1630 around the central large bead.

31. Using the same thread, attach three single beads 15° 553 in a semi-circle around the outside of the bead circle flower centre.

32. Using the same thread and beads, attach single beads on either side of the bead bud stems, using the colour image to guide you.

33. Referring to the three-dimensional elements in the bead embroidery gallery on page 48, work a beaded orchid with 10 beads in the first row of each petal. Use beads 15° 574 and light orchid beading thread.

TIP

Because your thread may be inclined to snag while stitching, consider making the three-dimensional beaded elements, but only attaching them to the fabric later.

34. Following the guidelines for attaching it to the fabric described in the general instructions on page 58, place it on the small circle depicted at the top of the head using the thread tails that are already there.

35. Using olive bead thread, stitch a single bead 8° 2035 in the space where the petals meet.

36. Bead couch six beads 15° 1630 in a semi-circle around the outside of the single large bead.

37. Using the same thread and following the instructions for simple flowers and leaves on page 61, work five-bead simple leaves radiating outward and downward between the orchid petals. Use beads 15° 459.

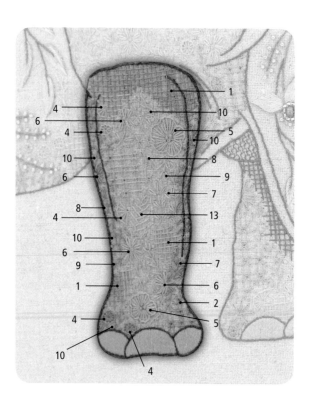

38. Using two strands of 613, pad the claws at the bottom of the leg with horizontal satin stitch.

39. Using a single strand of the same thread, work vertical satin stitch over the padding.

40. When you have completed the surrounding embroidery and working with a single strand of 844, outline the top semi-circle of each claw with whipped backstitch. The bottom will be taken care of when you outline the entire leg.

41. Refer to the freestyle stitching index to identify the numbered stitches in the colour image below left.

42. Use a single strand of 646 for the darker areas at the top and on each side of the leg, slowly moving to a single strand of 648 for the lighter, inner section of the leg. This requires that you work stitches in one or other of the threads in the same area as the two shades merge.

43. The lines down either side of the leg along with the outline around the entire leg are 2:1 whipped backstitch worked with 844.

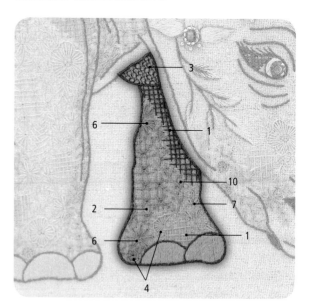

44. Continuing in the same way as the leg you have just done, use 844 couched with 646 for the diagonal trellis couching at the very top, following by single weaving shading done in 844 to create the shadow below that.

45. The remainder of the leg is worked with single strands of 646 and 648 using the image above as your guide.

46. The claws are worked in the same way as the leg you have just done, with padded satin stitch using 613.

47. Outline the top semi-circle of the two claws with backstitch using a single strand of 844.

48. Work the other outlines with 2:1 whipped backstitch using 844.

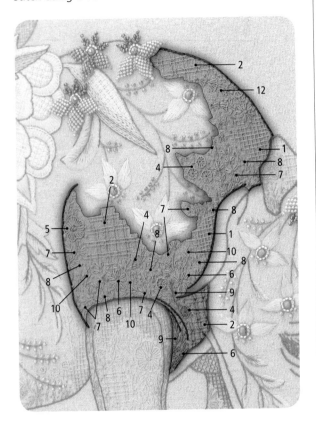

49. In the lower area immediately behind the left side of the face, work the freestyle stitching with a single strand of 646.

50. Thereafter, work the texture of the hide depicted in the image above with 648, leaving space for the Jacobean elements.

51. Work all the lines and outlines with 2:1 whipped backstitch using 844.

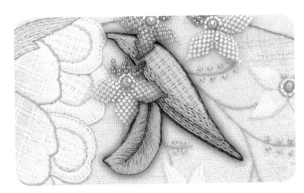

52. Moving to the Jacobean elements at the front of the body, fill the leaf on the left with diagonal long and short stitch shading that faces into the vein on both sides. Starting closest to the vein, use a single strand of 926 shading through 927 to 3348 on the outer edges.

53. Using the image above as your guide, work intermittent outline stitch to create shadow around the edge using a single strand of 924.

54. Using the same thread, work outline stitch down the vein.

55. Moving to the other large leaf and referring to page 72, fill the ovate section on the right with needle weaving texture no. 8. Use Finca Perle #12 3000 for colour 1, the warp stitches and #12 4799 for colour 2, the weft stitches.

56. Starting immediately adjacent to the tip of the woven section, work three rows of chain stitch backstitch combination down to the base of the leaf, finishing the second and third rows short of the base.

57. Use two strands of 3348 for the chain stitch and a single strand of 3346 for the backstitch.

58. Fill the rest of the leaf with rows of chain stitch backstitch combination using two strands of 3354 for the chain stitch and a single strand of 150 for the backstitch.

59. Outline the outside edge of the pink chain stitch with outline stitch using a single strand of 150.

60. Starting from where the pink ends, define the outside edge of the green chain stitch on the left and the woven area on the right, eventually meeting up with the pink, with outline stitch using a single strand of 3345.

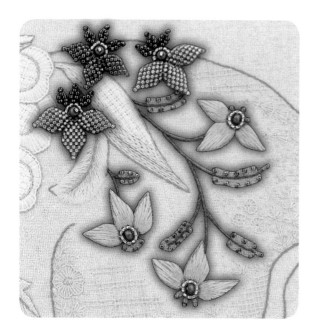

61. Using two strands of 648, pad the petals of the three-petal orchids with horizontal satin stitch.

62. Work single strand vertical long and short stitch shading over the padding using 3856 at the base of each petal shading up to 951 at the tip with a few stitches of 3836 shaded into the lighter tip.

63. Using the colour image above to guide you, define one side of each petal with outline stitch using a single strand of 3836.

64. Work the stem of each flower and the bead bud stems in whipped stem stitch using two strands of 3835.

65. Using a doubled-over single strand of 648 and following the guidelines for attaching a single bead on page 68, attach a bead 8° 2035 in middle of each flower.

66. Bring the needle up next to that bead and following the instructions for bead circles on page 58, work a circle of 10 beads 15° 1630 around the central large bead.

67. Using the same thread, attach three single beads 15° 356 in a semi-circle around the outside of the bead circle flower centre.

68. Using the same thread and beads, attach single beads on either side of the bead bud stems, using the colour image to guide you.

69. Referring to the three-dimensional elements in the bead embroidery gallery on page 48, work the beaded orchids as follows:

- The flowers on the right and lower left are worked with 12 beads in the first row of each petal. Use beads 15° 553 and dusty rose beading thread. Three five-bead simple leaves worked with beads 15° 459 and olive beading thread radiate out of the top of each flower.

- The flower in the middle is worked with 10 beads in the first row of each petal. Use beads 15° 356 and light orchid beading thread. Three five-bead simple leaves worked with beads 15° 459 and olive beading thread radiate out of the top of this flower.

70. Following the guidelines for attaching them to the fabric described in the general instructions and basic knowledge at the beginning of the bead embroidery gallery, place them on the circles provided using the thread tails.

71. Using olive bead thread, stitch a single bead 8° 2035 in the space where the petals meet.

72. Bead couch six beads 15° 1630 in a semi-circle around the outside of the single large bead.

73. Using the same thread and following the instructions for simple flowers and leaves on page 61, work five-bead simple leaves as listed above. Use beads 15° 459 and olive beading thread.

74. Referring to the gallery of embroidery stitches, fill the centre of the large Jacobean flower with woven trellis couching (*see* page 28).

75. Use two strands of 3856 for shade 1, a single strand of 3346 for shade 2 – the couching stitches – and two strands of 951 for shades 3 and 4.

76. When you have completed the surrounding embroidery, including the top leaves, come back to outlining this centre area. Starting at the base and working in a continuous line with a single strand of 3345, work whipped backstitch adjacent to the woven trellis couching.

77. With a single strand of 3347, work outline stitch adjacent to the outside of the whipped backstitch.

78. Moving to the four outward- and downward-facing petals, pad each one with horizontal satin stitch using two strands of 648.

79. Work long and short stitch shading over the padding of each petal.

80. Working from the base, use a single strand of 3354 shading through 151 to 951 at the tip of each petal.

81. Using a single strand of 951, work trellis couching with cross-stitch filling over the shading, lining up all the lines so that they seem continuous over the petals.

82. When you have completed the surrounding embroidery, outline each petal with whipped back-stitch using a single strand of 3350.

83. Starting with the two petals on the left and the three on the right, fill the centre of each with needle weaving texture no. 8. Use Perle #12 3000 for colour 1 and 4799 for colour 2.

84. Pad the outer edge of each petal with stem stitch using two strands of 951.

85. Work striped blanket stitch over the padding, fanning around as you go. Use two strands of 951 for the blanket stitch and two strands of 3856 for the small straight stitch in between.

86. Using a single strand of 3347, work outline stitch in the ditch between the weaving and the striped blanket stitch.

87. Using a single strand of 3731, work outline stitch adjacent to the outside of the ridge of the blanket stitch using the image above to guide you.

88. Pad the centre of the two bottom leaves with horizontal satin stitch using two strands of 648.

89. Work vertical long and short stitch shading over the padding, starting at the base with a single strand of 3856 shading up to 3354 at the tip.

90. Pad the outer edge of each leaf with stem stitch using two strands of Ecru.

91. Work striped blanket stitch over the padding, starting at the tip and working down on each side. Use two strands Ecru for the blanket stitch and two strands of 772 for the small straight stitch in between.

92. Using a single strand of 3731, work outline stitch in the ditch between the shading and the striped blanket stitch.

93. Using a single strand of 3347, work outline stitch adjacent to the outside of the ridge of the blanket stitch using the image on page 161 to guide you.

94. Starting from the left, fill the left side of the far left leaf with needle weaving texture no. 8 (*see* page 72) using Perle #12 3000 for colour 1 and 4799 for colour 2. Outline the outside edge with outline stitch using a single strand of 3345.

95. Fill the right side of this leaf with a chain stitch backstitch combination using two strands of 3733 for the chain stitch and a single strand of 3350 for the backstitch.

96. With a single strand of 150, work outline stitch up the vein continuing along the outside edge of the pink area.

97. Moving to the second leaf on the left, fill it with vertical lines of chain stitch/backstitch combination using two strands of 3347 for the chain stitch and a single strand of 3348 for the backstitch.

98. Outline the outside edge with outline stitch using a single strand of 3345.

99. Moving to the next leaf, fill the left side with needle weaving texture no. 8 using Perle #12 3000 for colour 1 and 4799 for colour 2. Outline the outside edge with outline stitch using a single strand of 3345.

100. Fill the right side of this leaf with chain stitch backstitch combination using two strands of 3856 for the chain stitch and a single strand of 951 for the backstitch.

101. When you have completed the section of weaving to the right of it, using a single strand of 3731, work outline stitch up the vein continuing down the outer edge to the bottom of the leaf.

102. Fill the top side of the leaf on the right with needle weaving texture no. 8 using Perle #12 3000 for colour 1 and 4799 for colour 2. Outline the outside edge with outline stitch using a single strand of 3345.

103. Fill the bottom section of this leaf with chain stitch/backstitch combination using two strands of 3354 for the chain stitch and a single strand of 3350 for the backstitch.

104. Using a single strand of 150, work outline stitch up the vein, continuing down the outer edge to the base of the leaf.

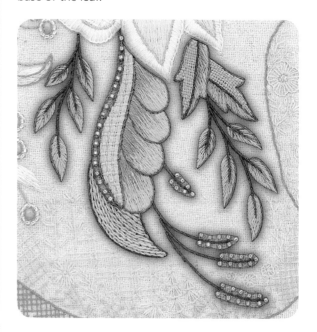

105. Starting with the central element, pad the four petals on the right with horizontal satin stitch using two strands of 648.

106. Work vertical long and short stitch shading over the padding starting at the base with 3733 shading through 3856 to 951 at the tip.

107. Define each petal with outline stitch using a single strand of 3731.

108. Fill the long area to the left of the four petals with needle weaving texture no. 8 (*see* page 72) using

Perle #12 3000 for colour 1 and 4799 for colour 2. Outline the outside edge with outline stitch using a single strand of 3345.

109. Moving to the tip of this element and starting on the bottom/outer edge, work three curved rows of chain stitch backstitch combination using two strands of 772 for the chain stitch and a single strand of 3347 for the backstitch.

110. Fill the remainder of the space with three more rows – or as many as you need – using two strands of 3348 for the chain stitch and a single strand of 3346 for the backstitch.

111. Define the outer edge with outline stitch using a single strand of 3345.

112. With a single strand of 3731, work whipped backstitch down the line that lies parallel to the woven section and running into the chain stitched section.

113. With a doubled-over stand of 648, attach single beads 553 at intervals in the space left between that line and the weaving.

114. Work the bead bud stems in whipped stem stitch using two strands of 3731.

115. Using a doubled-over single strand of 648 and following the guidelines for attaching a single bead on page 58, attach beads 15° 553 along each side and at the tip of each stem.

116. Moving to the leaf stems on either side of this element, start working the larger leaves above the stem on the right.

117. Fill the left side of the left leaf and the top side of the right leaf with single weaving using DMC Perle #12 927.

118. Fill the remaining side with diagonal long and short stitch shading using a single shade of 927 closest to the vein, shading out to 3348.

119. Using a single strand of 924, work outline stitch down the vein of each leaf.

120. Outline each leaf with outline stitch using a single strand of 3768.

121. The smaller leaves and stems on that branch and, also, the branch of leaves on the other side of the central Jacobean element are worked in the same way as you did on the face, using the same threads.

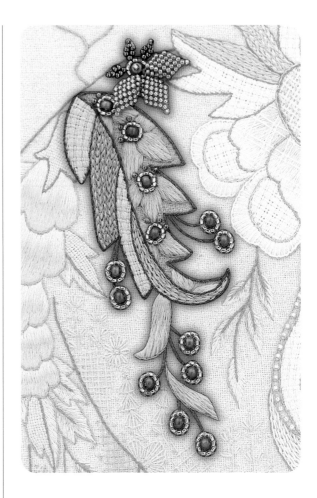

122. On the right of this leaf are 'cut off' orchids. Pad each petal or part thereof with horizontal satin stitch using two strands of 648.

123. Thereafter work vertical long and short stitch shading that starts with a single strand of 3856 shading out to 951 at the tip and including a few extra stitches worked with a single strand of 3836. Where necessary and using the same thread, work outline stitch on one side of the petal.

124. Before moving on, work the two petals below the main leaf in the same way using the same threads.

125. Work all the purple bead pod stems and the outline of the right side of the leaf with 2:1 whipped backstitch using 3835.

126. Using a doubled-over strand of 648, one bead 8° 2035 and 10 beads 15° 1630, create the bead pods in the same way that you worked the centres of the orchids on the face and the front part of the body.

127. Work the centres of the orchids within the leaf in the same way, adding single beads 15° 356 around the top of the bead circle centres.

128. Moving to the left side of the large leaf and starting at the tip, fill the first section with rows of chain stitch backstitch combination using two strands of 772 for the chain stitch and a single strand of 3346 for the backstitch.

129. Moving down the leaf, fill the next section with needle weaving texture no. 8 using Perle #12 3000 for colour 1 and 4799 for colour 2.

130. The space below that is filled with rows of chain stitch backstitch combination using two strands of 3347 for the chain stitch and a single strand of 772 for the backstitch.

131. The bottom section is filled with needle weaving texture no. 8 using Perle #12 3000 for colour 1 and 4799 for colour 2.

132. Outline the outside edge of each section of the leaf with outline stitch using a single strand of 3345.

133. Using the same thread, work outline stitch up the vein from base to tip.

134. The three-dimensional flower on the right of the leaf is worked with 12 beads in the first row of each petal. Use beads 15° 553 and dusty rose beading thread. Work the centre in the same way as the other flowers with bead 8° 2035 and six beads 15° 1630. Three five-bead simple leaves worked with beads 15° 459 and olive beading thread radiate out of the top of each flower.

135. Referring to the image below left and the freestyle stitching index, complete the tummy using mostly a single strand of 648, with only a small amount of 646 in the corner on the right, adjacent to the leg, and at the very base of about half the area as you move from right to left.

136. Work 2:1 whipped backstitch on the bottom outline using 844.

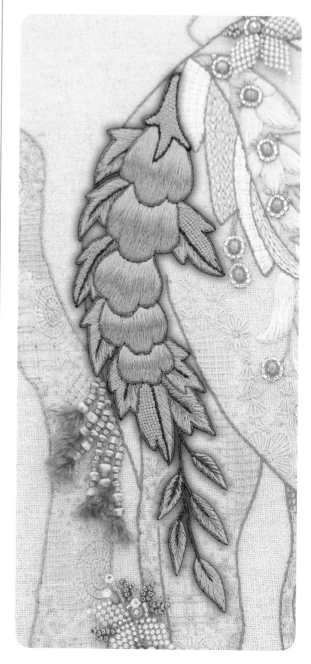

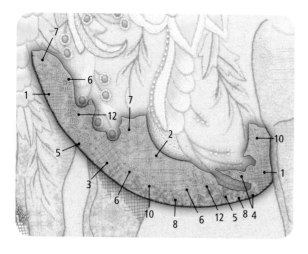

137. Fill the calyx at the top of this frond with single weaving using DMC Perle #12 927.

138. With the same thread, do single weaving in the top half of the single leaf on the top right and the third leaf on the left of the frond, as well as the large leaf pointing down at the bottom.

139. Fill the remaining half of those leaves, as well as all the other large leaves radiating from the frond with diagonal long and short stitch shading using a single strand of 927 shading out to 3348.

140. Work outline stitch up the vein of each leaf using a single strand of 924.

141. Outline each side of each leaf with outline stitch using a single strand of 3768.

142. The branch of small leaves coming out at the bottom is worked in the same way as you did on the face, using the same threads.

143. Pad each of the petals of the frond with horizontal satin stitch using two strands of 648.

144. Work long and short stitch shading over the padding with single strands of thread. Start at the base of each petal with 3856 shading through 3354 to 3733 at the tip.

145. Work an outline stitch around the outer edge of each petal with a single strand of 3731.

146. Finally, outline the calyx with outline stitch using a single strand of 924.

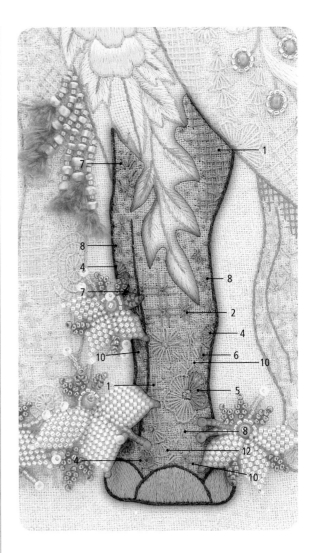

147. Complete that leg with reference to the image above and the freestyle stitching index. The lower central part of the leg is worked with 648 which blends out to 646 on the sides and at the top.

148. The claws are worked with 613 in the same way as they were in the front legs, outlined with a single strand whipped backstitch using 844.

149. The line up the leg and its outline are worked with a 2:1 whipped backstitch using 844.

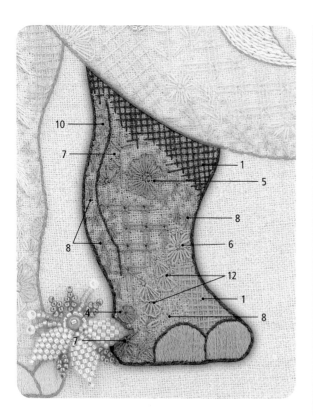

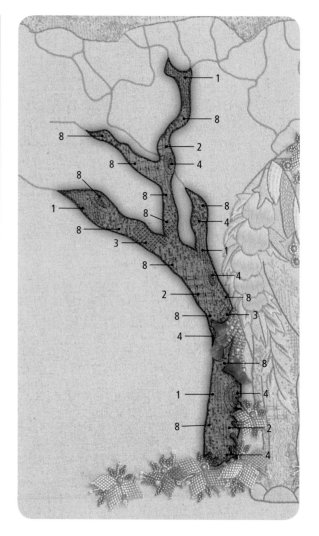

150. Complete the remaining back leg in the same way, referring to the image above and the freestyle stitching index. Use 844 at the top and 646 in the middle and on the left side, blending into 648 at the bottom and front of the foot.

151. The claws, outlines and line up the side of the leg are worked in the same way as before.

152. Using a single strand of Chameleon Rustic Brick, work the trunk of the tree with reference to the image above for the section to the left of the animal and below for the section above the animal. Follow the guidelines in the freestyle stitching index. Note that the buttonhole circles are two concentric circles. Work the outer circle first with the inner being worked so that the ridge lays over the raw edges of the initial circle.

153. When you get to the area of the tail, work the diagonal trellis couching over the area, semi-covering the lines. You will lay the tail over this trellis.

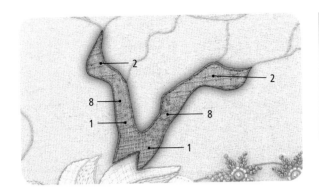

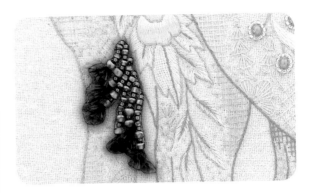

154. The outline of the trunk and the branches are backstitch worked with two strands of 611. Where the backstitch outlines the freestyle stitching, whip it with a single strand of the same thread. At the top of these sections of freestyle stitching, where both lines come together and continue as a branch, combine the two single whipping threads so that they become two strands. The stand-alone branches are whipped with two strands.

155. Using a doubled-over strand of 844, bead couch each of the lines that form the tail, with reference to the image above.

156. Start at the top by picking up a bead 15° 2210. Thereafter alternate beads 15° 2210 and 11° 4557 until you get towards the bottom of the line. At the end, still alternating with the size 15° bead, pick up one or two beads 8° 4557 instead of the size 11° bead. Finish with the size 8° bead.

157. Referring to the guidelines for bad hair day tufting on page 29, work five or six stitches at the end of each line of beads. When you snip the threads, don't be too neat. You want the fluff at the end of the tail to be a bit 'wild'.

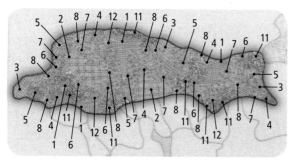

Left side foliage

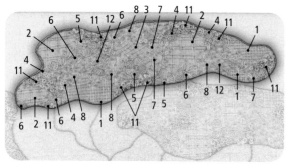

Top right foliage

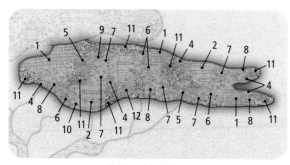

Bottom right foliage

158. Using a single strand of Chameleon Woodland, work the foliage of the tree with reference to the images above. Follow the guidelines in the freestyle stitching index.

159. When you have completed each area, thread up with a single strand of 3347 and work evenly. Spread single wrap French knots in between all the stitching except for the single weaving and the trellis couchings.

160. Outline each area of foliage with 2:1 whipped backstitch using 3835.

161. The three-dimensional orchids at the base of the trunk along with the simple bead leaves required for each flower are listed below. The colour of the beads and beading thread for the flowers are included in the list. For the simple bead leaves use olive beading thread.

162. Work the centre in the same way as the other flowers with bead 8° 2035 and six beads 15° 1630.

- Far left flower: 14 beads in the first row of each petal. Use beads 15° 642 and dusty rose beading thread. Three five-bead simple leaves worked with beads 15° 459 radiate out of the top of the flower with two more at bottom left.

- Second left flower: 12 beads in the first row of each petal. Use beads 15° 356 and light orchid beading thread. Three five-bead simple leaves worked with beads 15° 459 radiate out of the top of the flower with two radiating out on either side at the bottom.

- Third left flower: 14 beads in the first row of each petal. Use beads 15° 553 and dusty rose beading thread. Three five-bead simple leaves worked with beads 15° 459 radiate out of the top of the flower with two more at bottom right.

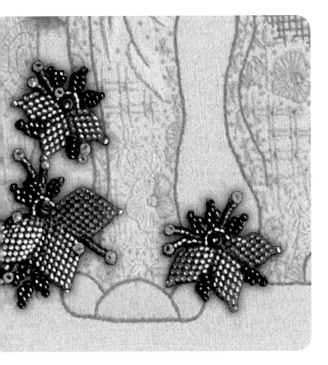

- Second right flower: 16 beads in the first row of each petal. Use beads 15° 642 and dusty rose beading thread. Three five-bead simple leaves worked with beads 15° 459 radiate out of the top of the flower with three more at bottom left.
- Far right flower: 12 beads in the first row of each petal. Use beads 15° 574 and light orchid beading thread. Three 5-bead simple leaves worked with beads 15° 459 radiate out of the top of the flower with two radiating out on either side at the bottom.
- Top flower: 10 beads in the first row of each petal. Use beads 15° 574 and light orchid beading thread. Three five-bead simple leaves worked with beads 15° 459 radiate out of the top of the flower with two radiating out on either side at the bottom.

163. Following the guidelines for attaching the flowers to the fabric, stitch each flower onto the dot depicted and work the centres.

164. Using cream beading, thread place stamens radiating out above and below each flower. Pick up between five and 10 beads 15° 650 – depending on the length you need for the stalk – and a single bead 11° 577. Return down the size 15° beads and back into the fabric.

Templates

Norman the tortoise (page 75)
Actual size: 207 mm (8$\frac{1}{8}$")
x 200 mm (7$\frac{7}{8}$")

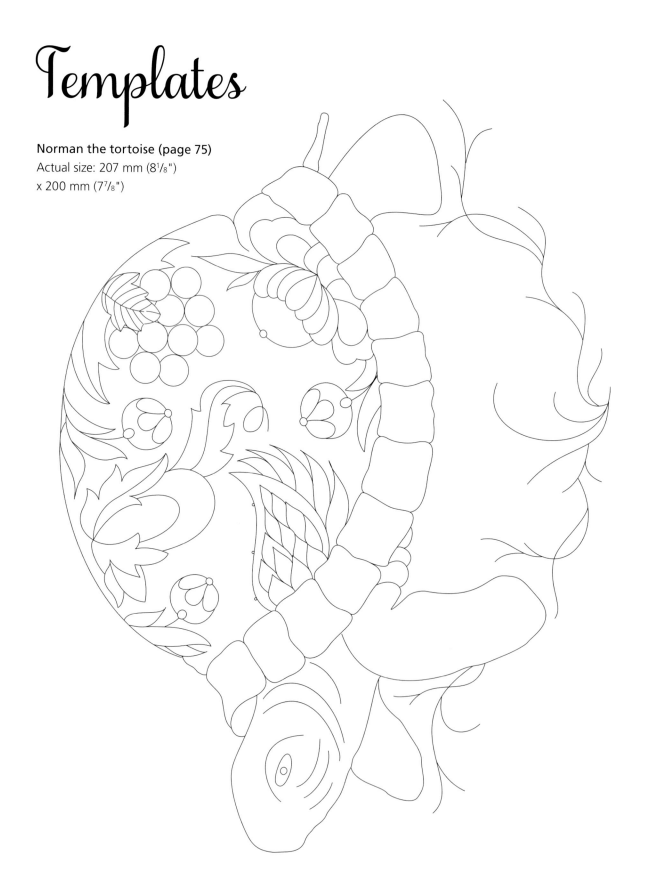

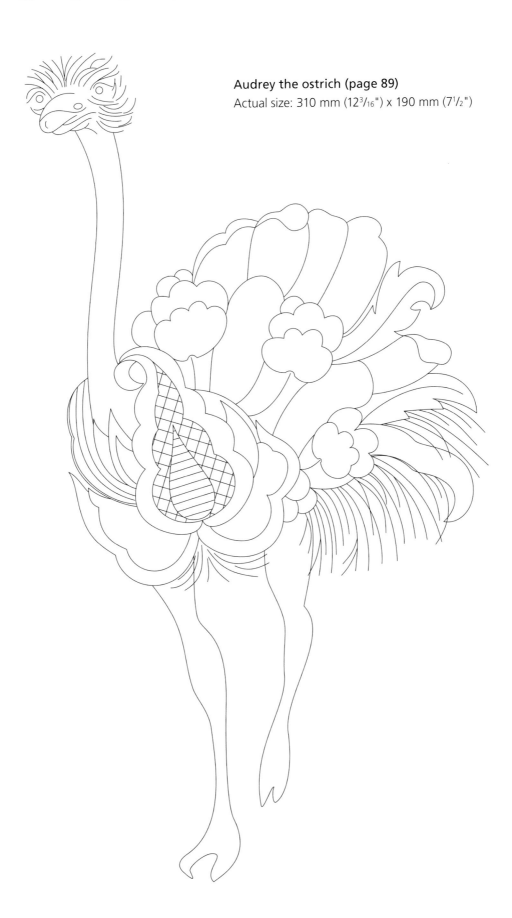

Audrey the ostrich (page 89)
Actual size: 310 mm (12³/₁₆") x 190 mm (7¹/₂")

Maureen the owl (page 101)
Actual size: 560 mm (22") x 340 mm (13³/₈")

Janet the snake (page 123)
Actual size: 270 mm (10⁵⁄₈") x 215 mm (8½")

Shirley the elephant (page 139)

Actual size: 315 mm (12^3/$_8$") x 255 mm (10")

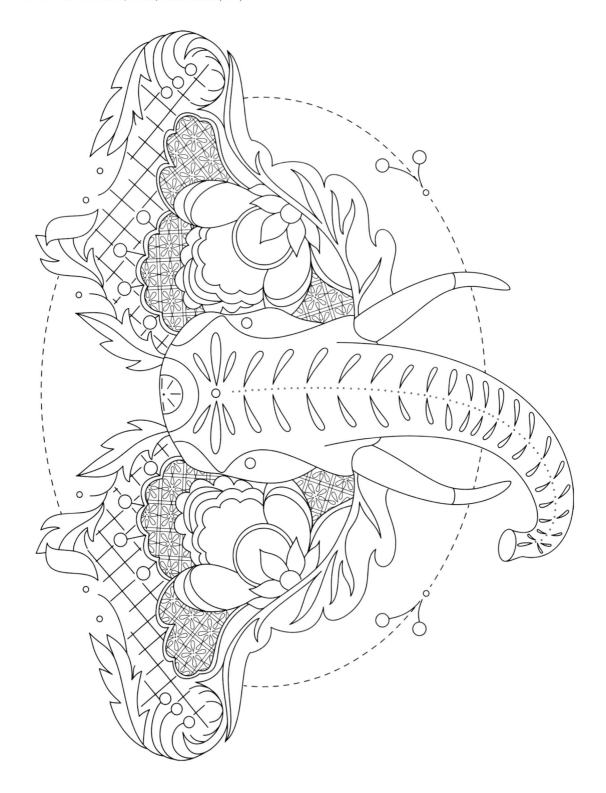

Roger the rhino (page 151)

Actual size: 430 mm (17") x 315 mm (12³/₈")

HAZEL *Blomkamp*

Hazel Blomkamp has dabbled with all the needlecrafts since childhood. When her children were babies she developed a passion for embroidery to break the tedium of life with toddlers, using it as her evening reward for having got through the day with her sanity intact. Her children are now young adults and she still embroiders in front of the television every night. She has been designing for the past 20 years. Preferring to design projects which appear to be traditional, she pushes the boundaries by introducing other forms of needlecraft into traditional techniques in everything that she does. Along with designing, she runs a busy website from home. She teaches at her home studio, in Pietermaritzburg, KZN, and travels throughout South Africa and the rest of the world teaching embroidery and fine beadwork. She is a regular contributor to South African, British and Australian embroidery magazines and an occasional columnist for South African *Stitches* magazine.